# Schlepping Across the Nile: Collected Stories

# Schlepping Across the Nile: Collected Stories

## Aaron Zevy

TUMBLEWEED PRESS, INC.

# COPYRIGHT

Edited by Jules Lewis
Copy Edit by Heather Karbi and Marianne Last
Cover Design by Tatiana Sayig
Book Design and Story Covers by Helen Prancic
Photographs courtesy of the Zevy Family
Stock Photos: 123rf.com, AJ Butler, Alamy, Around Egypt Tours, iStock.com, Lakewood Fogels, pixabay.com, and unsplash.com

ISBN: 978-1-7782017-5-2

Printed in Canada.

# DEDICATION

For my mother and father

I am the first born son of an Ashkenazi father and Sephardic mother. They were both born in Egypt and both kicked out in 1956. They ended up in Canada. These, almost true, stories, vignettes and memoirs tell the tale of growing up as a minority within a minority.

I tell people that the 'schlepping' in the title is a nod to my father's Ashkenaz side.

But that's not really true.

I never heard him say it.

I just think it's a funny word.

# CONTENTS

# SECOND EXODUS

This story begins with a phone call from my cousin Morris. It also begins with something I almost never do when getting a phone call from my cousin Morris.

I answer it.

Right away, I am reminded of the benefit of screening.

"You know what your problem is," he begins without even saying hello "I'll tell you what your problem is."

I don't say anything because I know Morris, who has quickly gotten over the shock of me having answered the phone, is going to barrel on.

"Your problem is you go out with Ashkenazi women instead of finding yourself a nice Egyptian Jewish woman. Somebody with similar history, food and culture. Someone you have something in common with."

Morris, I should mention, married a very nice Ashkenazi woman.

I say "You're right. I never thought of that." Which I thought might end the discussion.

But it didn't.

"I know of someone," he says." I have her number."

"Morris," I reply in what I hope is my sternest tone.

But then he says something which we both know carries a lot of weight.

"You might get a good story out of it."

Adele Harari and I spend the first thirty minutes of our date playing Egyptian Jewish geography. Not because we want to find people we have in common. But because we want to make sure we aren't cousins.

We're not.

Not really.

We then, because it is the middle of the Jewish holiday of Passover, gingerly probe our respective food restrictions and realize that although neither of us believe in anything, we both ask the waitress to remove the verboten croutons from our caesar salads. Morris is right. There is a lot of commonality.

"It's nice not to have to explain to someone what meggadara is," I say with a smile.

"I don't know," she replies "I like to play up the Egyptian thing. Men think it's exotic."

"Not so much," I say with a laugh.

"Especially this time of the year," she continues, ignoring my tease, "I have my own coming out of Egypt story. You must have one too."

"Of course," I said.

But I'm not sure I did.

My favorite part of the seder is L'dor Va Dor.

In every generation we are to regard ourselves as if we ourselves had gone out of Egypt.

I love that. Because this is when my mom would say "I did go out of Egypt."

My mother and father, my aunts and uncles, were once part of an 80,000 strong Jewish community in Egypt. Most left, or were kicked out, after the 1956 Suez Crisis. Their departure, often, like their forefathers, without having the time to wait for the bread to rise, is colloquially referred to as the Second Exodus.

So, there should be a story. But, growing up, it never occured to us to ask. It was just part of their history. And later, when my nieces began to take a real interest, my mother had forgotten many of the details and, more importantly was too hungry and tired to start recounting old tales.

So we were left with short recollections, a train ride, melted down jewelry, my Tante Lilianne being arrested, and scant details which often changed as the years went by. There was not much of a story.

Adele Harari, on the other hand, had a great exodus story. Her family owned a large store which sold kitchenware. Harari's was known all over Cairo as the place to buy high end flatware imported from Belgium. With his store about to be nationalized by the Egyptian government, Marcel Harari, Adele's grandfather, sold the store to his general manager, Achmed Mawfouz, a Copt who had worked in the store for nearly forty years, for ten cents on the dollar. The sale, which on the face looked more like a steal, came with the pledge from Mawfouz to smuggle the Harari family who, falsely accused of being communists, had been unable to get, by bribe or otherwise, an exit visa, out of the country. Mawfouz had instructed the Harari's to pack lightly and be ready to move at the shortest notice as he awaited notice from the Egyptian fisherman whose trawler would take them to Cyprus. The knock on the door came, the Harari's swear on a stack of bibles, when they were reciting Dayeinu. They stole out in the middle of the night with the clothes on their back. It was six weeks later, in an Israeli absorption camp, that Marcel Harari remembered that they had left without finding the afikoman that Harari had hidden in a loose floorboard in the dining room. He managed to send a message to his ex manager who went back to the Rue Roi Farouk apartment and retrieved the embroidered table cloth- the rats had eaten the middle matza- who then took a picture of himself holding the table cloth.

Adele Harari handed me her phone where she had, in her photo folder, a picture of the original photograph.

It was a good passover story.

At the last seder we ever had with my mother, who died peacefully in her sleep a week later, Rena, who had earlier dramatically rapped the Four Questions, decided to press her luck and ask again about our family's exodus from Egypt. She waited until after my mother had finished her plate of ashkenazi food which now graced our table every passover.

"Nona," she implored. "Tell us the story about when you left Egypt."

"It is ancient history." She said helping herself to a matza meal roll which, on day one we convinced ourselves almost tasted like the real thing "what do you want to know?"

"Is there a story?" She asked.

"The story," she said "is we were in Egypt. Then we came to Canada and made a life for ourselves."

"That's all?" Asked Rena.

My mother didn't say anything for a few seconds. At first I thought she had fallen asleep.

Then she shrugged her arthritic shoulders and said

"What else is there?"

In the months and years following my mother's death, I made an effort to contact my aunts and uncles and cousins both on my mother's and father's side in order to glean more details about how they left Egypt. Everyone, it turns out, was fired on the same day. Their bank accounts were frozen and my Tante Lilianne did spend some time in prison. My father, though born in Egypt, was Ashkenazi and somehow managed to land himself a passport. Everyone else scrambled to get a laissez passer and then find a country which would take them in. Some made it to Switzerland, some to France, and some, like my father, to Italy. Eventually most made it to displacement camps in Israel- the only place that had really opened their borders. All described their life in Israel as being really hard. Perhaps it is the passage of time but none of their stories were told with any bitterness. If anything, they all remembered their life in Egypt as halcyon days. It had been a place which was good for the Jews. And then it wasn't. In their mind, they had had a good run. Most ended up in Montreal, Canada. I don't suppose any had ever even seen snow before. They had children and dressed them in snow suits and scarves and mittens. They shoveled driveways and went tobogganing. Im not sure how they did it.

It was not a story, like Adele Harari's, you could dine out on. But it was their story. Their story of having made a life for themselves. For their children and for their grandchildren. Their story was one of looking forward and not backward.

And really, what else is there.

# HOME MADE CAKE

My mother grew up in a large apartment on Rue Ismail Pasha in the Cairo suburb of Heliopolis. Some time after the 1952 officers' revolution which overthrew King Faruk and brought Gammel Abdel Nasser to power, the street was renamed Rue Bagdad. Streets often change names in the Levant, depending on how the political winds blow.

The apartment was well situated. There was a stop for Cairo's above ground metro only a few metres from the house. There was a florist on the ground floor. The Kashmir Cinema, which showed movies in Arabic, was walking distance, and the open-air Normandy Cinema, which had American and Italian films graced with both Arabic and French subtitles, was only one stop away. The fruit store and butcher were around the corner, and what food you could not get sometimes came to you on the street. This was

7

primarily *ful medames*, the fava beans which were the staple of Egyptian cuisine and culture, which would arrive, by horse- pulled cart, in a huge copper pot every morning at 7.

But the crown jewel of the neighborhood was across the street. It was a French bakery, a patisserie, owned by a Greek family. It was called, if you can believe, Home Made Cake.

Now Cairo in those days was not only an ancient city with a storied past but was also the epitome of what we now refer to as a melting pot. Arabs, Greeks, French, Armenians, Brits, Copts, Turks, and Jews represented but a handful of the nations which filled the city streets. That melting pot was accompanied by all the respective languages - including English. But when my family spoke about Home Made Cake, I could not fathom a place with such a generic English name. Instead, I heard it in Arabic -

*Om Met Kek*.

As in "Ya wallad, je n'ais jamais manger un croque en bouche aussi bon que a Om Met Kek." My boy, I have never eaten as good a *croque en bouche* as I did at Om Met Kek.

My Tante Nandi, who lived down the road on Boutros Basha Gali, became misty eyed when talking about it. This from a woman who was famous for her own desserts. Her baklava and konafa were a thing of legend in our family.

"Ronnie," she would say, "your mother lived across from heaven. You can't believe how good the pastries were at Om Met Kek."

Om Met Kek.

Pronounced very quickly. With no pause between each word. As if it were only one word. It sounded like all the other Arabic names and expressions. I mean, in what world would there be a French patisserie in Cairo called Home Made Cake? I don't speak Arabic. I have learned a few words and phrases. I was pretty sure that Om meant mother. I just thought it was someone's name. Like the

Swiss baker Groppi whose famed cafe with the eponymous name was the place to be seen for the pashas, beys, and doyens of Cairene society.

My father lived in north Heliopolis. My uncle Henri, my mother's brother, was his best friend. Every Sunday morning he would come for breakfast, and every Sunday he would stop at Home Made Cake before going back home in order to pick up pastries for his own family.

My mother came from a family of seven brothers and sisters. All but one, my Tante Gracia, who moved to Brazil, eventually landed in Montreal, Canada after being effectively thrown out of Egypt after the 1956 Suez Crisis. Although neither of my grandmothers, both of whom made the Atlantic crossing with their children, ever learned a single word of English, my father, mother, and all my aunts and uncles spoke it very well. My Tante Lilliane even worked as a French/English translator. My Tante Odette, who says she was so bad at math that she didn't qualify for the more academically rigorous Lycée Français, went to an Anglo/Arabic school. Tante Nandi became a bank manager and had to be proficient in French and English. Both my father and uncle Henri went to university and learned in English and Arabic. Although accented, they spoke English very well, with a rich vocabulary and proper grammar. I might be belaboring the point but I just want to make it clear they all spoke English very well.

But every time they spoke about the patisserie on rue Ismaili Pasha I never, not once, heard the words Home Made Cake.

Only Om Met Kek.

Of all the food my family was nostalgic about after leaving Egypt, the one they missed the most was not Egyptian at all. It was from Home Made Cake. And while they insist that everything in the store, which even had a convenient take out window, was absolutely delicious, the piece de resistance was the éclair. The only debate was if they preferred the chocolate or the coffee flavored filling. My Uncle Henri claimed they were the best eclairs in the world. His proclamations, delivered as if sermons from the mount, would often be a source of amusement for my father. But in this case, my father was a disciple. They were the best eclairs he had ever had. No éclair, not even the Duke de Gasgogne French bakery, could match those from their beloved Heliopolis patisserie.

To hear them tell it, the marvel of the éclair was not only the pastry and the filling - it was the size. The éclairs, they said, were huge. I was pretty sure it was a fisherman's tale rolled up in dough - the eclairs became bigger as each year went by.

"We used to cut them in three," my mother told me more than once.

I remember bringing a box of éclairs to the Egyptian poker group at the Hemispheres in Hallandale, Florida. They were, to be fair, from Publix, but they looked good. They thanked me for my gift but not as effusively as I had hoped. Only Tico had the guts to speak his mind.

"Ronnie," he said, "you need to understand. We ate éclairs from Om Met Kek. These are like a kick in the balls."

Om Met Kek

I had gone 60 years thinking that was what it was called and would have happily, inchaalah, gone another 60. And I would have were it not for a conversation I had with Tonto.

Tonto, in this case not the Lone Ranger's side kick, but the nickname my niece Danna has anointed to my Tante Odette. A nickname which the entire family has adopted. I called her to see how she was doing.

As usual she answered "Zay el zift merci," which means I am shit, thanks.

Which, as I said, is her default answer but this time she could lay some legitimate claim. She was recovering from her second broken hip and was cooped up in her apartment because of the pandemic. Her only guest was her son, my cousin, Morris, who brought her food and took her on short outings. So desperate was he to find her entertainment that he had taken to reading her some of my stories. Morris said I had gotten some good laughs, but instead of a compliment I got a complaint. Why did I not write more stories about Heliopolis and their lives in Egypt? I promised I would in my next book. I would even write about the great chocolate éclairs at Om Met Kek.

And she said "What?"

And I said "Om Met Kek."

And she said "De quoi tu parles?" What are you talking about?

And I said "The bakery across the street."

And she said. As clear as day. She said "Home Made Cake."

I said "Home Made Cake?"

She said "Oui. Home Made Cake." Again. Clear as day.

I said "I thought it was an Arabic name. Om Met Kek."

And then she laughed. But good. She couldn't get a word out she was laughing so hard.

When she could get a word out it was only to say *"majnoun,"* which is 'crazy' in Arabic.

Then she said "Yalla bye," and hung up.

Ten minutes later the phone rang.

It was my cousin Morris.

"Hey Ron what's up?"

And I said "Just go ahead and say it."

"Say what?" He replied innocently.

"Just get it over with," I said.

"Ok," he said, "now listen closely. I am going to say it slowly:

Home

Made

Cake."

And I said "I would kill for a chocolate éclair." And he said "Yeah, me too."

# TEN HOUSES

When I get back home from my walk I find my mother in the kitchen making her famous stuffed peppers.

This would ordinarily have given me considerable pleasure.

Except my mother has been dead for five years.

It is a bit of an existential crisis and one which I should confront immediately, but I really do love those stuffed peppers.

And not only has she come back from the dead, but she has brought spices and condiments with her.

So I decide to wait it out.

The peppers are as good as I remember, even better, no rust on her cooking at all. She has made a simple salad of lettuce, tomatoes, and cucumbers, oil and vinegar dressing, and has toasted a couple pieces of pita. We eat in silence. She makes a passing remark about my hair being too long but we mostly just eat without talking. I have missed these Egyptian dishes and am enjoying the combination of flavours and nostalgia. I am clearing the plates and loading the dishwasher when she finally announces the real reason for her visit.

"We did not let you go out for Halloween during the FLQ." She says, referring to the terrorist organization which in the fall of 1970 had kidnapped a British diplomat and murdered a Quebec politician, causing the prime minister, Pierre Elliot Trudeau to invoke the War Measures act.

"You have to change it."

So now I get it. She has not come back to cook. She has come back to edit.

She is referring to a new story I am working on called 'Ten Houses'. The plot hinges on me being allowed to trick or treat, but mostly to collect money for UNICEF, at ten houses on our block on the afternoon of Halloween during the October Crisis in 1970. I find a valuable coin in my Unicef box and have to decide whether to return it to its rightful and unsuspecting owner. It is a morality play which Jules, my actual editor whose culinary skills I am not privy to but who has the editorial distinction of actually being, you know, alive, and I have worked back and forth on. I think it turned out quite well.

"It's just to help the plot, mom," I explain. "It narrows down my search to ten houses. I needed a reason why I was only able to go to a few houses."

She holds up her hand in some sort of Egyptian 'don't go there' gesture, momentarily lifting it from the cup of Turkish coffee she has made from a 'canaka', a coffee pot, which I do not own.

"*Jamais de la vie,*" she exclaims. "That would never happen."

And then, putting an exclamation mark on it, she says in Arabic "*bokra fel mish mish.*" Which literally means 'when apricot season comes' but figuratively means 'when pigs fly'.

I try to explain how the stories mix fact and fiction but she is not having any of it.

"*Jamais de la vie!*" She repeats.

She then asks if I have any chocolate ice cream. I shake my head no. She arrives with peppers, stuffing, and Turkish coffee but no ice cream?

Then my father, who has been dead for fifteen years, appears in the living room, wearing his customary socks and sandals, holding a bowl of ice cream for me and a small cone for my mother.

He looks well all things considered.

"Show me the story," he says. I hand him the sheets. My father, though not really a fan of fiction, revered books and writing. He would set emotions aside and examine it rationally and pragmatically. I watch him read my story. I had a funny bit in the second paragraph and although it does not elicit a big laugh I do get a smile. I like that.

Then he looks up and says "It is nice to read about my old friend Taki." I nod my head. Taki was a colleague of my father's from work. I brought him into the story as the coin collector who happened to be at the house when I got back. He is the character who tells me the coin is valuable. Taki did not really collect coins. I just made that part up. But my father lets it go. He finishes reading and looks up.

"It is a morality play," he says.

I say "Yes."

"The boy discovers a valuable coin in his Unicef box and now has to decide if he gives it back."

"Exactly," I reply.

"It is a good story," he says.

I say "Thanks."

Then he says "Icarus," wagging his finger, "you flew too close to the sun."

"But I..." I stammer.

"That scene makes no sense," he says. "Nobody is going to believe we let you go out during the October Crisis."

"It was just ten houses," I argue.

"No." He shakes his head. "Look." He holds up the story and reads from it. "My mother was in charge of our costumes. But really, she was in charge of us not having costumes because she insisted my sister and I wear our winter parkas over any costume we had."

"Does that sound like someone who would let you go out of the house while there were kidnappings and murders?"

I shake my head no.

"That one inconsistency harms the entire story."

He is right. My buddy Harold Rosen would never believe it. There was no way I would have been allowed out. The story did not hold water.

I say "It is the 50-year anniversary of the October Crisis. And this year parents also have to decide whether to allow their kids to go trick or treating. I thought it would make a good story."

"Yes" he says. "It would make a good story. But this is not that story."

I say "Ok. I will change it."

He says, "Good. And maybe get a haircut too."

And then he and my mother disappear.

I never finished the story. Jules and I went back and forth a few times but I could never quite figure it out. By then I had a Goldfarb and Lewberg story which had a few good laughs so I eventually forgot about it altogether. Halloween came. I'm not sure how many kids went out. I can tell you nobody came to my house. I had bought some chocolate bars just in case but knew I was just going to eat them myself. But I didn't want chocolate bars. What I really wanted was a bowl of my mother's Syrian soup. A nice bowl of *chamd* with a scoop of rice.

I power up my laptop and open up a word document.

"This is the story about the time my mother let me go out and play in the middle of winter with wet hair."

Then I set the table and wait.

# JAFFA ORANGES

Photograph © SolStock / iStock

When I was twelve I was chosen to represent our Montreal suburb, Dollard-des-Ormeaux, for its under-13 soccer team.

Which is why, up until very recently, whenever the subject of soccer came up, there was a very good chance I would say, "You know, I played on a select team when I was young."

Select.

But this story is not about my soccer skills or about glory days.

It is about the lessons of history.

The biggest difference between playing in the house league and playing select soccer, outside of the quality of play, was that the house league was played at our local park, which was three blocks from our house, while the select games were played on soccer fields throughout Montreal and its suburbs. Places like Beaconsfield, Kirkland, Lake of Two Mountains, and Verdun.

It meant the fathers, it was always the fathers, of the players were responsible for carpooling the kids on Sunday mornings. They split up the shifts and it worked out to something like once every three weeks.

My father took his obligatory turn and loaded me and three of my teammates into his brown 1970 Chevy Impala. Once at the soccer field he would set up a small folding lawn chair under a shade tree and read his book, usually a volume of history, until the game ended. He would look up, bemused, if he heard a loud cheer and even once returned my wave when I ran by.

At the end of the game, he would respectfully, even a little solemnly shake coach McPherson's hand, as if they had just reached an accord on an arms treaty, pile the same crew into the Chevy, and drop them off at their respective homes.

He would ask me if it was good - c'était bien? - never if we had won, and I would then give him a quick recap. He was a big believer in physical fitness and I think he was pleased to see me running outside in the fresh air, but the concept of winning and losing was not one he deemed worthy of his attention. I know he played basketball when he was young but I had never seen him watch or talk about sports. When the newspaper arrived, he handed me the sports section.

I found the entire ordeal more than a bit stressful. Besides the lawn chair, the book, the sometimes socks with sandals, my father drove painfully slow - the Chevy had never once visited the passing lane - and he insisted on playing classical music the entire time. I begged him to play pop music or no music at all but the conversation was a nonstarter. The best compromise I could come up with was he would not turn up the volume for the canons during the 1812 Overture. He did enjoy taking us to Dairy Queen though, he loved his ice cream, and that would usually help temper the embarrassment of the slow driving and the Tchaikovsky unless one of my teammates made the mistake of getting into the car with an unfinished cone still dripping in his hand. He wouldn't say anything. Just slowly and sternly wag his finger no. My father was a tall man who had played basketball as a teen. Years later, NBA star Dikembe Mutombo had a trade mark 'not in my house' finger wag when swatting away balls headed for the basket. My friend Steve Kahansky, who had been on the receiving end of my father's finger wags plenty of times, would always say that Dikembe stole it from Marco Zevy.

All in all I managed to survive carpooling and it had been a great summer, until the Sunday when it was our turn to be in charge of the other team obligation: providing the halftime oranges.

In theory, it should have been a very simple task. Fill a cooler with ice. Cut the oranges. Put the oranges in the cooler.

We had a cooler.

We had ice.

We had oranges.

Well, we did have oranges. But we didn't have the oranges everyone else had. They had California navel oranges. It is the most eaten orange in North America. Readily available in any and every supermarket. But the Zevys didn't have California navel oranges. No. We had Israeli Jaffa oranges.

Could we maybe get regular oranges I wondered out loud.

Jaffa oranges, my father proclaimed, are the best oranges in the entire world. Your team is in for a treat.

He was not wrong. Jaffa oranges were delicious. But I was just trying to fit in. And I would have argued a little bit more to get my way if I didn't have to deal with another, more pressing, issue.

My father refused to leave the peels on.

From week one, all the oranges were cut in four, with the peels intact. At halftime, the players would grab a slice or two and suck on them. Then discard the peels, as the juice ran down their chins, into a big green garbage bag. That's how we did it. Every week. Every single week. But now my father wanted to remove the peels of the oranges, the Jaffa oranges, and offer up peel-free slices.

I asked him why.

He shrugged his shoulders and then answered in English. It was a language he spoke fluently. One of the seven languages he spoke. But it was a language he never ever spoke with his children, fearing, presciently, they would forget how to speak French, their mother tongue.

He said "Because we are not animals." He then handed me a knife and I stood next to him at the kitchen counter, removing peels, making slices, and putting them into plastic bags.

The score was 1-0 for our opponents at halftime when Coach McPherson asked me to go fetch my father. We had started eating the oranges and nobody had said a word about the type of oranges or the fact that they had no peels but my heart was still pounding as I went to get my father. He was reading a Churchill biography. I told him the coach wanted to speak with him. He placed a bookmark in the book, dog earing was for heathens, got up and followed me back to the team bench.

Coach McPherson said "Mr. Zeevy, I've got a wee bit of a family emergency. I wonder if you could coach the lads for the second half."

I have no idea why Coach McPherson asked my father. He had never expressed an interest in soccer. Had never even watched more than a minute of a game. The other fathers knew the game. They knew the team. They knew the players. But maybe those solemn handshakes had made an impression. I was hoping, praying, he would just bow out and let one of the others take the helm, but my father had a strong sense of duty and always doing the right thing.

My father spoke English fluently. Still, it was always strange to hear him in English. Unlike my Uncle Henri, whose English sounded like the late Egyptian president Anwar Sadat, my father's accent, although undeniable, was harder to place. Like a wine tasting, you could detect hints and bouquets of Cairo, of Jerusalem, of Paris, of remote and exotic towns and villages. He now addressed me and my teammates in that accented English. Using a stick he had picked up from the ground, he began to make scratchings in the dirt. If I had a stick I would have made a hole big enough to crawl into. He did not know anybody's name so he just pointed and said "You". As in "You go here." "You go there." It was a very offensive and aggressive 2-3-5 alignment. Completely different than the way we usually played. He didn't speak again in the half other than to make substitutions. He made sure everyone played. We scored three goals and won easily.

We didn't speak after the game. Together we carried the cooler, it had leftover oranges because we had brought too much, back to the car. We went back home. He drove as slowly as ever, played Mozart at a low volume, and we even stopped for our regular Dairy Queen.

My mother greeted us at the door and asked how the game was.

I said "We won 3-1!" Then, pointing at my father excitedly, said "He was our coach!"

She looked up at my father with a surprised look and asked what I had wanted to ask.

"What do you know about soccer?"

He shrugged his shoulders and, still speaking English, said:

"The 1956 Hungarian national team. The Magyar formation."

Then he walked into the house wearing his socks and sandals and carrying his Churchill biography.

# EGYPTIAN SOUP

My nieces and I play a drinking game at our Passover Seder. As I am both wifeless and childless, in addition to lacking the requisite maturity, I sit in the children's section directly across from my brother who sits at the head of the table with the rest of the adults.

The Seder, as some of you may know, is actually a religious ceremony where drinking is not only allowed but mandated as part of the reading of the Haggadah. In fact, we are required to drink four glasses of wine—two before dinner and two after. But we decided to supplement the religious rites by adding a twist of our own. We would take a drink when triggered by specific words or actions of our fellow Seder participants. In other words, our family and close friends. I don't really want to throw any of them, or my nieces for that matter, under the bus by divulging any of those triggers but suffice it to say the word "colonoscopy" alone has gotten them drunk long before the pickled brisket is served.

I would like to think I am the cool uncle. At least I was until a few years ago when it became abundantly clear that I had, unbeknown to me, transitioned from playing the game to being one of the designated triggers.

My drink-inducing utterance was complaining about how I preferred the Sephardic Egyptian/Syrian food which graced my parents' Seder table over the Ashkenazi swill I was now forced to eat.

Turns out, I said it a lot. Maybe not as much as colonoscopy, but a lot.

Chinese food is just food to the Chinese. The same can be said of the Egyptian food we ate growing up. For us, it was just food.

My nieces call it yellow food because much of it is made with saffron and turmeric.

It was food with strange names. Arabic names. The conversation was in French but the food names were almost always in Arabic.

"Ronnie, *tu veux un autre morceau de marshi?*"

Marshi.

Zucchinis or large peppers stuffed with rice and meat. Flavored with lemon and garlic. It was my favorite. And my aunts knew it.

My brother loves *warak enab*—stuffed vine leaves. The Greek call them *dolmades*. But they serve them cold. Not the same. Not civilized.

Some of the pronunciations varied depending on whether you were from Syria, Lebanon, or Egypt. My Tante Nandi made deep-fried torpedo-shaped balls of bulgar wheat on the outside and minced meat on the inside. They were heavenly. Would make an atheist believe in God. Our family called them *kobbebah* but my cousin Tita and her family, who grew up in Lebanon, call them *kibbe.*

The delicious side dish of lentils and rice with fried onions then topped with yogurt is *megadra*—soft *G*—or *megadera*—hard *G*. Our family used the hard *G*.

One of the many traits I picked up from my mom is the need to tell strangers I know where they are from. That we are from the same place. Arabic could not be spoken without my mom piping up. "Yes," she would say. "*Masri*," using the Arabic name for Egypt.

A few months after she passed away, I was in Starbucks when I heard two people speaking to each other in French. It was French but it was with an Egyptian accent. For us, it is unmistakable. I would like to say my mother's spirit took me over when I addressed them but I think it was all me.

"Let me ask you something," I said. "Do you say megadra or megadera?" They were startled but didn't miss a beat.

"Megadera," she confirmed.

"Ah. Us too. Masri?"

"Iwa, yes, Masri."

And then I left with my tall latte.

Vegetables are hard enough for kids to eat but made worse in Arabic. *Fasoolia* was a green bean stew. *Bizella* were peas. The harsh-sounding *charshuf* were artichokes. *Bamia*, never my favorite, was okra.

Those, and others, were the names of the food from my childhood. My Jewish childhood. But I never saw them in the works of the great Jewish writers like Bellow, Roth, and Richler. We were the other Jews. These were our words, our foods. Nobody else we knew ate them or had even heard of them.

My brother-in-law, Jamie, an Ashkenazi Jew from Montreal, tells the story of the speech he gave at his and my sister Danielle's wedding. He listed the food his new mother-in-law had introduced him to. It wasn't a bit. He wasn't making a joke. All he did was repeat the names of the food in Arabic. He was amazed that each item elicited a huge laugh from my cousins and me. Because we never heard those words outside of our own dining room. Not in books, not in TV, not in film.

That's not to say we lived in a totally insular bubble. We would very occasionally go for pizza—my father repeatedly reminding the waitress no pepperoni, and to please bring his beer with his food. On special occasions we might go to Ponderosa Steakhouse. And I remember when the first McDonalds, serving 22-cent burgers, opened in our neighborhood. But the Zevys, by and large, did not go out to eat. We ate at home. Or we ate at one of my aunt or uncles' houses. If we ever ate dinner at someone's house who was not an Egyptian Jew, I have zero recollection of it. I think because it never happened. Maybe my parents had friends. Maybe they went to their houses for dinner. But I don't think so.

Lunch was a different matter. I walked to school and came home for lunch. *The Flintstones* were on at 12:00 pm. Sometimes a classmate invited me to their house for lunch. I almost always said no. In part because I did not want to feel obligated to reciprocate, and in part because I had a pretty serious fear of Campbell's Cream of Mushroom Soup.

The Jewish religion says a boy becomes a man when he turns 13. I think a boy becomes a man when he starts eating creamed soups; in my case, I was 27. Lunch was invariably soup and a grilled cheese sandwich. Crusts cut off.

The best possible soup was Lipton's Chicken Noodle Soup. It was a packet you put in a bowl and poured boiling water on.

Delish.

The second best possible soup was Campbell's Tomato Soup. It was not good but it was edible. Often it would include some sort of cracker.

The worst possible soup was Campbell's Cream of Mushroom (I am not going to talk about the time Mrs. Wilson served Cream of Asparagus. She left her husband a week later so am pretty sure she was just acting out). I would eat it and pray to God I did not throw up.

I had been to Stevie Sheen's house for lunch twice (Lipton's Chicken Noodle Soup—Mrs. Sheen is surely in heaven now), and once after school for chocolate chip cookies. I couldn't put it off any longer. I didn't want to be that guy.

I went to speak to my mom.

"I invited Stevie Sheen for lunch tomorrow."

She didn't look up from the TV.

"Okay."

I stood in front of the TV, blocking her view.

"Just soup and grilled cheese sandwich. Maybe some chips."

She waved her arms, imploring me to move away from the TV. My father, who was on the recliner reading a volume of Will and Ariel Durant's *Story of Civilization*, lowered his glasses and looked up to see what was the commotion disturbing his post-dinner tranquility. He looked at me. Then he looked at his wife. Then he looked at me again. But he didn't say a word.

"Mom, Lipton's Chicken Noodle Soup. Okay."

I saw my father smile. He was enjoying this.

"Lipton's?" My mother asked. "With the boiling water?"

"Yes. It is very good. All the moms serve it. All the Canadian moms. The kids love it."

But my mom wasn't buying it.

"Don't worry, Ronnie. You want soup. I'll make you soup. I'll make you a wonderful soup."

This was not good.

My mom made a lot of soups. But she was talking about a "wonderful soup". That meant, oh god, it meant one of three soups. All three were a problem. The least problematic was a Syrian chicken soup called *hamud*. Hamud means sour in Arabic. It is a chicken soup with celery, potatoes, lemon, garlic, and mint leaves. It often includes meat balls called *kibbe*. It is topped with white rice. To be clear, it is my favorite soup in the world. My nieces absolutely love it. My sister-in-law, who incidentally is a fantastic cook, makes her own and it tastes like it came from the streets of Cairo. I ordinarily frown on taking pictures of food but every single time I eat hamud I take a picture of the bowl and post it in our family chat. That is how much I love it. Most of you reading this are no doubt saying, that sounds yummy, why is this soup problematic? It is because you are not a 10-year-old Christian (yeah, I said it) boy living on the West Island of Montreal who has been weaned on a steady diet of Campbell's Soup. The problem with the soup is it mostly looks like chicken soup. So, even with advance warning, you take the first spoonful expecting chicken soup and are accosted instead with chicken lemon garlic soup. Believe me, it is delish. But tell that to Stevie Sheen.

The second most problematic soup was lentil. In Arabic it is *adz*. My mother's maiden name is Ades and it is a derivative of that word. Yes, yes, I know. Lentil soup is the bomb. I know that. You know that. But Egyptian lentil soup is a brown concoction which frankly looks like... well, I'd rather not say. I can say it makes Campbell's Cream of Mushroom Soup look like a walk in the park.

The most problematic soup is the nuclear option.

My mother would never. I mean she could never. But the thing was, it was her favorite soup. It was my father's favorite soup. But no, she could never. I am talking about *molokhia*.

To start with. Nobody can really agree on how to spell it.

*Molokhia.*
*Mulukhiyah.*
*Mulukhiyyah.*
*Molohiya.*
*Mloukhiya.*

To be fair, it is a transliteration of an Arabic word. Think of the strong guttural "*ch*" sound common in that language.

It is an Egyptian soup made with the leaves of the *corchorus olitorius*—commonly, ironically, known as Jew's mallow. It is very popular in Egypt and very much associated with the community of Egyptian Jews.

My community.

Go online and Google it. You will find videos on how to make the best Egyptian molokhia. You might even find it on the menu at a New York Egyptian restaurant. But, back in the day, nobody had ever heard of, much less tasted, molokhia. It existed only within the very close and closely knitted walls of the Egyptian Jewish community.

At this point, I have to try and convey how much my parents and my aunts and uncles and all their Egyptian friends loved (and still love) molokhia. It wasn't a staple but rather a treat, because, like many of their favorite foods, it required lengthy manual preparation. I can't pretend to know or remember but the leaves had to be cooked and dried? I really don't know. Only that it was considered a special treat. And the argument and debate about who made the best molokhia is still ongoing. My late Aunt Fernande was generally thought to be the undefeated champion.

The other thing I need to tell you about molokhia is that it is—how should I say this?—well, let's just say it is an acquired taste.

To begin with, it is visually unappealing. Today, it is de rigueur to be slurping down kale smoothies but back then nobody, except for my family, was eating what amounted to green leaf soup.

Then consider the consistency. Some of you will be comfortable with the use of the words viscous or glutinous. The rest of us will just say slimy. And not in a good way. The soup, heavily flavored with garlic, is tempered somewhat with a generous scoop of white rice. It is a concoction which, by all reasonable measures should elicit sounds of retching but, with my family, produced contentment and pleasure.

My suspicion is they are eating not soup, but nostalgia.

You can't, in good faith, serve it to anyone who has never dipped a toe in the Nile.

She couldn't.

She wouldn't.

I think my mom saw the panic in my eyes. She got up from her chair, went to the kitchen and came back holding a packet of Lipton's Chicken Noodle Soup. People think it is from my father, but I think I got my sense of humor from my mom.

I sighed a breath of relief and said thank you.

"Grilled cheese?"

"With the crusts cut off. Your mother is a Canadian."

My father went back to his book.

Crisis averted. I went to bed and then to school the next day without a care or worry in the world.

That was my mistake.

I let my guard down.

See, *The Flintstones* were on from 12:00 pm until 12:30 pm. Then lunch. Lipton's and grilled cheese. All good. What I hadn't accounted for was my mom would never allow a guest, even 10-year-old Stevie Sheen, to sit in her house for a half an hour without giving them a snack. I mean, we weren't Ashkenazis.

I had forgotten about the pre-meal appetizers.

In our house, in any Jewish Egyptian house, there were always three good options. All delicious. All tasty.

The first was *lahm bi ajeen*. It was a meat pie. The speciality of my Tante Odette. It was like a mini pizza. Delish. Not a problem at all.

The second is *sambousek*. Puff pastry which can be filled with cheese or with meat. My mom added pomegranates to her meat sambousek. Whether cheese or meat, her sambousek were unbelievable. Huge crowd pleasers. She served them to her dying day. She had them ready frozen and fresh all the time. Her grandchildren flocked to eat them. They were culinary rock stars.

No, sambousek would not be a problem.

The problem was the third option. A circular savoury biscuit with sesame and coriander. It is delicious. It is addictive. A favorite amongst friends and family.

A fantastic treat with an unfortunate name.

Stevie and I were watching *The Flintstones* when my mom came out with a tray and pleasantly and innocently asked Stevie if he would like some *kaak*.

I don't know what became of Stevie Sheen. And I can't really blame him. He was a 10-year-old boy after all. But that year, I was known as the boy who served kaak for lunch. It would be many years before I invited someone over again.

This year for Passover I am sitting right next to my brother at the head of the table. My sister-in-law has made matzo ball soup, two different types of kugel, her mother has brought her famous pickled brisket, roast chicken, potatoes, salad, and she has even made rice for the Sephardics. The food is delicious. The guests are bestowing well-earned compliments. Dinner is buffet style and I get up and help myself to another piece of pickled brisket. Add a little mustard. It really is good.

Really.

But what I wouldn't do for just one piece of my Tante Nandi's kobbebah.

Looks like they will have to drink another glass of wine.

# LE CHINOIS

At some point in this story, I am going to insult some of my best friends in the world. I will say, somewhat defensively, my intention is not to insult them but rather to praise my late uncle, Henri Ades.

But my defense will ring hollow. Because, in truth, I do mean to insult them. Anyway, that's not for now. It is a little bit later in the story. I just wanted to give you the heads-up.

The story, I think, is about poker.

I was taught to play poker by my older cousin, David, on the stoop of an apartment hotel on St. James Street in Atlantic City.

There is a picture of me on the beach during those years and I am alarmingly thin. Like a Romanian gymnast.

If I would have to guess, I would say that I am eight.

Our family drives to Atlantic City, New Jersey, for a two-week vacation on the fabled beach which once hosted the Miss America pageant.

It is almost unfathomable for me to understand how my father, who later in life grew to despise even a fifteen-minute ride to the shopping center, would have, year after year, undertaken this long journey.

Atlantic City, back many years before the casinos, was beach in the morning and boardwalk at night. Our lodgings had a TV and this was where my sister and I first watched *Love, American Style* and *The Mary Tyler Moore Show*. We did not have cable at home. The vending machine in the motel across the street—not where the Jews stayed—is where I tasted my first Mountain Dew. The beach and ocean were a mini paradise, with the ice cream man trudging his cooler on the hot sand, bellowing the virtues of 'fudgie wudgies.'

At night, our parents would sit on the rows of benches near the Steel Pier, an area they called La Palmyra. After the beach town in Syria decimated by ISIS? No. That doesn't seem right. Hold on, let me call my Tante Odette.

Ah, so it turns out La Palmyra was an open-air cafe in the Heliopolis district of Cairo. My aunt peppers me with questions as to why I want to know this ancient history. But I am in the middle of this story so don't have time to chat.

Yallah.

Bye.

The benches on the Steel Pier serve as a time capsule of younger years. For most of my aunts and uncles, their time in Cairo, as almost all youthful times, were halcyon days. We are given our allowance in order to play skee-ball and mini putt while they just sit on the benches eating and spitting sunflower seeds and enjoying the breeze from the ocean.

My father, although born in Egypt, is the lone Ashkenazi in the bunch; he exhales contentedly and says it is a 'mechayeh.'

I look up the word in order to confirm. It is a feeling of joy and pleasure. Like taking your girdle off at the end of a long day.

How can you derive pleasure from doing nothing? From sitting, eating sunflower seeds?

How old am I before I understand how great that is? Am I fifty? Could I have been a fool for that long? It seems very likely.

We come back from skee-ball and try to negotiate a few more dollars for soft ice cream.

"*Mange de la pastec*," urges my mom as she takes out a Tupperware of cut-up watermelon from her beach bag.

Pastec is french. She doesn't use the Hebrew or Arabic word for watermelon—*avatiach*.

French, Arabic, English and Hebrew are sprinkled in most sentences. It is the language of the Egyptian Jews.

A polyglot dance trotted out at rapid speed.

Pay attention.

Don't let your mind wander.

Do you want to be embarrassed like my younger brother who, when asked in his advanced French class what the French word for garbage was, quickly shot up his hand and exclaimed, to the understandable wonderment of Monsieur Lebeq, "Zaballa?"

Zaballa.

Because in our house, the chore was *"va faire sortir la zaballa."* All in French except for the last word. The Arabic word for garbage.

Zaballa.

And la zaballa meant it was in the feminine.

I mean, seriously.

I did say this story was about poker. And it kinda is. But I first want to talk about class. About wealth. And about social standing.

Many of you will already know that the famed board game Monopoly was based on the streets of Atlantic City. If not, then there you go. Fun fact.

Not all the streets. Park Place, for example, is clearly New York City. And the railroads. Well, the railroads are the railroads.

Our kosher hotel, my father called it a pension—a guest house—was on St. James Place.

Don't cheat.

Don't look it up.

Do you know what color group St. James Place belongs to?

Orange.

Now orange isn't the purple of Baltic Avenue. But it sure as hell isn't the yellow of Ventnor or the green of Pacific! We are in good company. Between Tennessee and New York. But we know our place. We don't let our britches get too big.

I grew up understanding I was a kid from St. James Place. I knew my place. In time, I turned out to be the asshole who thought he owned all of Boardwalk. But that was later. Much later. For now, I was the youngster playing poker with his cousin.

So we sat on the stoop, after first crossing the street, inserting the American quarters into the magical vending machine and getting our ice cold Mountain Dew, and played poker.

It would have been draw poker.

No wild cards.

Played for, I don't know, maybe pennies?

Did my sister play? Did his sister? Two-handed poker doesn't seem like much fun, but neither does playing poker with our sisters.

My cousin David does not play poker now. In fact, that may very well have been the only time he played. Buying and selling companies seems to be enough gamble for him. But he got me hooked.

I still play a lot of poker. I have played in card rooms in Atlantic City, Las Vegas, Los Angeles and Florida. I have played the casino in Leicester Square in London and the Champs-Elysées in Paris. In Prague I played in a game in which the only English words any of the players knew were call, raise and fold.

I also play in a lot of home games. The monthly $20 buy-in, no-limit hold 'em tournament at my friend Harold's house. It might be the worst poker game in North America. After 20 years most still ask if flush beats straight. The players, all very early risers except for me, have trouble keeping their eyes open past 10:00. Decisions are made not on the relative strength of a hand but on wanting to go to bed and reluctance to buy in for a second $20.

My friend Bernie reminds me we played for much bigger stakes when we were sixteen. He is right.

My brother has a rotating dealer's choice game almost every month, and I am a first alternate at my friend Downtown Darren Brown's game where, in the last hour, they play the same three-handed Guts game we played when we were 16.

My friend Karen has included me in her couples doctor game although I am neither coupled nor a doctor. The stakes are low, and I often play a hand in the dark—without looking at my cards. Her husband, Oscar, to this day, does not believe me when I say I am in the dark. He simply can't conceive of someone being that dumb. Karen's friend Shawn plays in the doctors game. In addition to being a pediatrician and poker player, he is a golfer and we have become friends. He invited me to his own home game.

All the players in this game are Chinese. Some, ironically, are from Singapore, where I lived for two years for my last two years of high school. They were surprised I recognized the distinctive Singlish accent. They order in food from a local Thai restaurant.

Though perhaps not very politically correct, I call this game the Chinese Game.

The stakes were high and the games were wild.

One of the crazy, wild games we play is called The Last Picture Show. Named after the movie with Cybill Shepherd.

It was a high-low game which changed depending which cards got turned up. And then they played an extended version where you could buy an extra card at the end.

It was crazy.

It was more than a little complicated. So much so, that when I tried to introduce it to my group, they gave up trying to understand after 10 minutes.

But that is not, as Arlo Guthrie said, what I came to talk to you about.

I want to talk about the poker game played in the card room of the Hemispheres building in Hallandale, Florida.

It was a game played by a group of Egyptian Jews between the ages of 82-92. It was a $10 buy-in and they used plastic poker chips they had bought at Walmart. The bets were by color rather than denomination. As in, I bet two reds and one blue.

They played, for reasons that are still a mystery, counterclockwise. My Uncle Henri was the king of the game and, despite the fact he was my former boss who had fired me three times, I loved playing with him. He had an aggressive, bullying approach and loved to bluff. Many of the players like my Uncle Henri had been playing since they were kids. And their nicknames were still the same. In fact, I often did not even know their real names. My uncle loved to tease Tico—whom I later learned was called Albert. Sometimes, Madame Giselle played with us and if she won a hand against Tico, my uncle would taunt him unmercifully.

*"Elle t'as baiser, Tico. Elle t'as baiser."*

You probably didn't learn that in French class.

It meant:

"She fucked you, Tico. She fucked you."

Tico would look up at me and say, "Ronnie, I'm getting killed here."

They would tell stories of the old days.

La Palmyra.

Sometimes, if I was lucky, I would be treated with a story about my father.

"He knew every public bathroom in Cairo."

I, in turn, would regale them with stories of the poker room in the casino.

"How much did you win, Ronnie?"

Did I inflate the numbers?

Okay. Maybe I did.

My uncle would have loved to have gone to the casino. But, by then, he was nearly blind. We would have to call out the cards on the board.

*Trois de pique.*

*Valet de couer.*

He only needed to be told once.

They played wild-card games and my uncle loved to learn new variations.

One day I told him of the game I played in the Chinese poker group.

"*Mais c'est un peux difficile.*" It's a little difficult.

"What is it called?" my uncle wants to know.

"The Last Picture Show," I reply.

"Show me," he commands.

"Henri. Forget it. The kid says it's difficult. We are too old to learn new games."

"Let's try one hand," my uncle would say with a twinkle in his eye.

The insults fly. In Arabic and French.

Your mother's... better left unsaid. Doesn't translate well.

But Henri is the king of the table and he gets his way.

The first hand does not go well. Neither do the next three or four. They can't follow the different games and they give up on the low part of the split pot altogether.

It is an unmitigated disaster.

My Toronto friends from the round table gave up after 10 minutes. Why would I expect more from these aging Egyptian Jews? "It's okay, Ronnie," says Tico. "We are too dumb for this game." Okay. Yallah, follow the queen.

It rains the next day and my golf game is cancelled. So I head down to the rec room to play cards with the Egyptians. When it is my turn to deal, I call out 7-card stud.

Deuces wild.

Easy game.

When it gets to my Uncle Henri, he calls out, "Le Chinois."

We look up. What game is he talking about.

"Ronnie's game from yesterday. From his Chinese game."

"No, Henri. No."

Henri stands firm. "My deal. My game. Le Chinois." And then, adding salt to the wound, he says, "Extended."

Our cousin Sammy wins a huge pot with six Queens. When it is his turn to deal, he calls out, "Le Chinois."

And so, for nearly a year, the only two groups in the entire world who played The Last Picture Show were my Chinese friends in Toronto and the octogenarian Egyptian Jews at the Hemispheres in Hallandale, Florida.

My parents are no longer alive. My Uncle Henri has also passed away. My Tante Odette stays in our old condo in the winter. I visit her from time to time. She makes me Egyptian food from the old days. Dessert is cut-up watermelon.

*Ne mange pas las pastec avec tais mains,*" she admonishes me. Don't eat the watermelon with your fingers.

I sometimes arrive early in order to beat the rush hour traffic. She is usually downstairs in the card room playing quatorze with the other ladies. Sometimes, there is a poker game.

"Ronnie, come play with us," urges Tico. "I am getting killed."

I recognize most of the faces but it is not really the same without my uncle. But I take a seat and pull out a $10 bill.

"Okay. I'll play a few hands. What's the game?"

"Le Chinois," says Tico in the most matter-of-fact way.

"Extended?" I ask.

"Of course," he says. Looking at me as if I were a fool. "Extended."

# YORKDALE

Photograph © Vadim Guzhva / 123rf.com

So here's how it usually goes.

I walk into the Rosens' unlocked house and Nida makes me some sort of sandwich. If I'm lucky it is some pressed chicken with hummus and the bread isn't more than two days old. Nida knows better than that. I wheel Harold to the table before pouring myself a glass of the last of their orange juice.

I mean that's on them. They know I am going to come by.

I eat my sandwich and regale Harold with some story of a woman who doesn't want anything to do with me.

At first Nida pretended not to pay attention but now she just makes herself a cup of coffee and finds a comfortable place to sit and listen.

I can't blame her.

Who doesn't love a taste of someone else's misery in the middle of the afternoon.

I then wheel Harold back to his spot in front of the computer, kiss him on the forehead, making sure not to kiss him where Handleman might have kissed him, put his baseball cap back on and head towards the door. Just before I reach the door I turn back and say, "You need anything?" And then Harold says, "We're good."

That's how it usually goes

It works for me.

This time I say, "You need anything?" and Harold says, "Actually, I need a favor."

I do an about-turn. Sometimes he needs his one leg lifted over the other leg in a certain way. It usually takes me about seven tries to get it right. You'd think he'd learn.

So I say, "What do you need?" Am looking down to see which leg needs crossing. But it isn't a leg. This is what he says:

"I want you to go to Yorkdale with me tomorrow so I can buy Gili a new mattress for her birthday."

Yorkdale is a shopping center. I imagine it is a bit like what hell might look like.

Although I suspect hell has better parking.

"You want me to go mattress-shopping tomorrow at Yorkdale?"

Harold says, "Yes. You would be doing me a big favor." I see Nida fighting a smile. She is enjoying this. She is saying to herself, "That's right, come over and drink the last of our orange juice."


I arrive at the Rosens' house the next day at the appointed time. This is what you can say about me: there's always an even chance I don't show up. But if I do show up, it is going to be on time.

I walk in the door and pray that Jonathon has shown up to take my place. Jon is his next-door neighbour and good friend. He is the resident handyman and go-to fixer for these types of things. But no such luck.

Harold is waiting for me in the hall. He is freshly shaved. He is wearing his shabbos clothes.

He says, "This is going to be fun."

For the first time in my life, I think of striking a man in a wheelchair.

It was actually the second time I have ever wanted to strike Harold. The first was over 35 years ago. I had gone to spend the weekend at his family cottage in the Laurentians—the Quebec cottage country a little more than an hour from Montreal. Carl, his father, had made us dig irrigation ditches. That night I got a phone call from a woman I knew. A woman I wanted to know better. She was also up north with a friend. Did we want to meet for a drink? Harold, who had the week before gone on all of one date with a woman—to be fair, it turned out to be the woman he would eventually marry—the woman we were now about to buy a mattress for—but we had no way of knowing that at the time— shook his head and spoke the words which caused me unspeakable ire, grief, and anger.

"I'm spoken for."

And now "this is going to be fun" is a close second.

It takes me a few tries to get the wheelchair up the ramp into the van. I finally figure out I have to back it in. Harold of course knows this but all of a sudden his MS has affected his tongue. Not a word out of his mouth.

I strap him in as best as I can. It doesn't seem right. It is like building an IKEA bookshelf and having 20 leftover pieces. I give the wheelchair a shake.

"Is this secure?" I ask.

He says it is good.

It doesn't feel good.

Fucking Jonathon!

I close the van door and shuffle towards the driver's door. A blast of wind hits my face. It is freezing. Makes sense. It is February in Toronto. I reopen the sliding van door. Harold is not wearing a coat.

"You're not wearing a coat," I say.

"I don't need a coat," he replies.

"It is February," I say.

"We are going to the underground parking. We have a handicap sticker. We are going to park right next to the elevator. We are taking the elevator to the store. I don't need a coat."

Once a lawyer. Always a lawyer.

With my luck, I am pushing the wheelchair in the mattress department of The Bay and we run into somebody we know. Word gets back I took Harold to Yorkdale without a coat. I need that like I need a hole in the head.

I say, "Wait here."

He says, "Where am I going to go?"

Once a comic.

I go back to the house and find what I think is a blanket. Later, I would realize it is a rug. But that was later. I grab it. Open the sliding door and wrap it around Harold's shoulders. Not great. But it would have to do.

I ease the van out of the driveway and head towards Yorkdale. I should take the Allen Expressway but I don't feel all that comfortable driving the van. Plus I have a handicapped religious Jew wrapped in what I later learn is a Persian rug tethered unsecurely in the back seat.

So I take the side roads.

The side roads have a lot of stop signs.

I think a big van like this requires a hefty stomp on the brakes in order for it to come to a full stop. But it turns out the brakes are hair-trigger.

Every stop sign, Harold and his chair lurch almost all the way into the front seat.

It's like a ride at La Ronde.

I curse Jonathon under my breath.

I finally get the hang of the brakes but by then we are already in the parking lot. Harold was right. Perfect spot right next to the elevator.

I open the sliding door.

Harold says, "It's a good thing I am already paralyzed." He is having the time of his life. Only thing which would make it better for him is if I threw up.

I can't figure out the strap. All of a sudden it is more secure than Alcatraz. I think about just cutting it with my Swiss Army knife. I think about just abandoning him here in the parking lot. And then the clasp just unclicks and we are both free.

The elevator takes us right to the mattress department of The Bay. We have the place to ourselves. A saleswoman makes her way to us. Very slowly. She is a short grey-haired woman with wire-rimmed glasses hanging on her neck. She is not a young woman. She looks like she may have been here since the store opened. She looks like she may have been here since mattresses were invented.

Her name tag says Marge.

She asks if she can help.

I say, "My friend," I point to Harold, "is in the market for a mattress."

Harold has done his research. He wants a queen-size Sealy. Firm. Marge says she has just the thing. And it is on sale. "Please follow me." I get behind Harold, unhook the safety lock, and start pushing. Marge is walking so slowly that I twice have to stop suddenly for fear of clipping her heels.

"Here we are," she says. "The Sealy Performa. Queen size." And I say, "It is on sale."

Harold wants to know if it is firm.

He wants it firm.

Gili likes a firm mattress.

Marge says it is firm.

Harold now says to me, "Lie on it. Tell me if it is firm."

"You want me to lie on it?"

Harold says yes.

So I slip off my shoes and lie on the mattress. I am staring at the ceiling of the mattress department at The Bay.

I get off the mattress and put my shoes back on.

Harold asks if it was firm.

I really couldn't tell. But I want to get the hell out of the mattress department at The Bay.

I say, "Yes. It was firm."

I can see that Harold is not convinced. But he says, "Okay."

Then Marge decides this is a good time to kick me in the balls.

She says, "You know, you really should lie on it yourself. After all, you will be sleeping in it."

Harold says, "That's not a bag idea." No typo there. Harold likes to say bag instead of bad. He thinks it is funny.

I look at Marge. She doesn't look strong enough to lift her glasses. I look at Harold. I curse Jonathon.

Marge, to her credit, has picked up on my panic. She says, "Let me call Hector from shipping." She reaches for the phone.

Harold looks up to me. He is smiling.

"This," he says, "is going to be fun."

Marge says, "How are you going to pay?" Harold says Visa. His wallet is in his back pocket. It still has his old driver's license.

33% off. Marge wasn't kidding about the sale.

Marge asks if we want to take it with us or have it delivered. Delivery is $50 extra.

I say delivery.

I may have shouted.

Marge says fine. Then she whispers conspiratorially, "I'm going to waive the delivery charge."

She is giving us the wheelchair discount. I am going to take Harold car-shopping with me next time.

Addresses are proffered. Signatures are scribbled. I can see the light at the end of the proverbial tunnel.

Marge gives us a smile and gleefully claps her hands.

"Perfect. Delivery on the 15th. Do you prefer 10:00-12:00 or 2:00-4:00?"

I don't know a lot of people's birthdays. But I know Gili's birthday. I know it because it is on Valentine's Day.

The 14th.

I say, "The 15th is no good. His wife's birthday is on the 14th. Has to be the 14th."

Marge looks at her ledger.

She looks at it for a long time. For a minute there I think she may have fallen asleep. Or died.

She looks up and has a very sad face. It looks like she might cry.

"There are no trucks on the 14th but, hold on. Well, yes. I guess. Maybe. I can get it to you after the last run. It will arrive just after 8:00 pm. Still no delivery charge."

Marge is now very happy with herself. Until Harold says, "No, we'll take it now."

Now I look like I am going to cry.

I turn to argue but I see his face. It is the same face he has when I ask if it is okay if I use a milk dish with my burger. He isn't going to be convinced.

I take Marge aside and tell her we are going to need Hector again.

Now, those of you who know me have figured out that I have already tipped Hector $50 for helping lift Harold out of the chair, onto the mattress, back on the chair, then back on the mattress because he just wanted to make sure one more time if it was firm enough, and then back on the chair.

So yeah. Hector is up 50 and he is about to be up 50 more.

I get Harold back into the van and we meet Hector at the loading dock.

Harold says, "Hey, Hector."

Hector says, "Hey, Mr. Harold."

Meanwhile I am freezing my ass off.

It is a shit show.

Hector explains how he intends to tie the mattress on the roof of the van. I nod my head but he could be explaining string theory.

I hand him another 50 and now I am Hector's assistant for the next 20 minutes. After five minutes, Hector understands he has to talk to me like a five year old.

We get the mattress on.

I can't feel my toes.

I have no idea how we are going to get the mattress off the roof but that will be on Jonathon.

I am done.

I take the side streets home.

I jam the brakes at every stop sign.

We eventually get back to Harold's house.

And I would pull into the driveway.

But I can't.

Because there is a truck in the driveway.

From Sleep Country Canada.

The mattress store.

Seems like Gili bought herself a new mattress for her birthday.

# APRICOT SEASON

The only thing I really remember coveting growing up was the Hot Wheels Race Track with the loop de loop.

It was in bright orange plastic. I already owned two or three Hot Wheels cars. And Stevie Sheen had two of his own.

But we didn't have the track. I asked my mother.

She said, "Ask your father."

So I asked my father.

He was doing his paint by numbers on the patio near the garden. He said it relaxed him. I asked if he could buy me the Hot Wheels Race Track.

This is what he said: "*Inchaalah*." *Inchaalah* means God willing. God willing.

I just wanted the Hot Wheels Race Track. To paraphrase Tina Turner, what does God have to do with it?

Inchaalah was not bad. Inchaalah was not a no. Inchaalah still gave one hope.

"*On va voir*" was also hopeful. It meant we'll see.

"*Dieux est grand*" was also in the inchaalah family. Any reference to God meant you never know what could happen. It wasn't bad. But it wasn't great.

"*Ne me derange pas waled*." A mix of French and Arabic—don't bother me son—meant your timing was bad. Real bad.

In my house, there was always still hope until one of my parents invoked apricots.

"Can Stevie and I take the bus downtown on Saturday night and then a subway to the Montreal Forum so we can see the Canadiens?"

To be clear, I wasn't stupid enough to ever ask for anything which began with me getting on a bus—as if my mother would ever allow that—but the response for that kind of request would be "*bokra fel mesh mesh*."

Which translates to, "When apricot season arrives."

As best as I, my brother, my sister, and all my cousins could ascertain, apricot season almost never arrived in Cairo.

And it never ever arrived in Montreal. Bokra fel mesh mesh. Translated. That's a hard no. Translated: When pigs fly.

But here's the funny thing about apricots.

Whenever my cousins and I would ask our parents for a toy, this is what they would say.

"Barbie doll?"

"GI Joe?"

Go ahead and fill in the blank for any desired toy: "_____?"

"Do you know what we played with when we were growing up? We dug a hole in the ground and played a game with discarded mesh mesh (apricot) pits."

Mesh mesh.

Again with the apricots.

I call my cousin Monica and ask her, "What game did your mom play growing up?"

She doesn't miss a beat. "The game with the mesh mesh pits."

I call my cousin Morris. He says the same.

I leave a message for my cousin David. He texts me back the next day. Mesh mesh pits. Seems like a lot of people were playing with apricot pits.

The rules of this game were never clear. Pits were thrown. Pits were picked up. Was it like jacks? Were there points? Nobody seems to know. In a world where sisters competed to be best at everything, nobody seemed to brag about their mesh mesh pit prowess.

But, despite the fact they could not really remember how to play, every time we asked for a toy, they reminded us of this hole in the ground with the discarded mesh mesh pits.

My father bought me the Hot Wheels Track. Not, however, before first declaring the whole endeavour was *"de la folie fourieuse"*— madness.

Stevie Sheen and I played with it for a while. We made elaborate tracks running in and out of the house. The loops were cool though. Eventually we lost all of the cars but one and then one of the main bridge track pieces broke. Stevie and I went back to playing Stratomatic baseball and we boxed it up. I think we eventually sold the one car and what was left of the track at a block yard sale. I think we got fifty cents for it.

For a while my sister and I saved our apricot pits. We kept them in an old olive jar we hid behind the can of lupini beans in the cupboard. I am not sure what we were planning to do with them. Play, I guess. We had gotten to about ten or eleven pits when my mother discovered them.

She asked if we were saving them and my sister and I both sheepishly shook our heads no. It was ridiculous. We had rooms full of toys.

"One game," she said as she ran the mesh mesh pits under water. "Your mother was the best."

I looked it up. It turns out apricots are only harvested two weeks a year in Egypt and were very hard to come by in Cairo. The ephemeral nature of the season gave rise to the expression.

Which leads me to ask this question: if apricots were such a rarity in Cairo, where the hell did they get all those mesh mesh pits?

# SILVER TWEEZERS

Photograph © Sergey Ryzhov / 123rf.com

I have started, more by accident than anything, collecting stamps. I had been thinking about writing a short story about a character who tries to impress a woman by getting his face on a stamp. It turned out though that you could order customized stamps with your face on them from the post office so it sort of made the idea a little less compelling. But by the time I found out, I had already bought a few books about stamp collecting and even ordered a few packs of stamps from Amazon in order to get started. I was now going to collect stamps. I went to my friend David's house and he showed me some of his Israeli stamps. I recognized many as stamps my father had collected and it brought back some warm memories. David asked me what I was planning to collect. Was there some sort of theme or category? I said I really didn't know. Maybe stamps from places I had lived in or visited he suggested.

And I said yeah, that might be a good idea. We had lived in Singapore for 2 years and I was interested in the history of the region. So I went back home and started looking up stamps from Singapore and from Malaysia. I wasn't looking for anything specific but then I stumbled upon the twenty-five-cent Malaysia. I knew that stamp.

This is a picture of the twenty-five-cent stamp from Malaysia. If you look closely, you can see the year. 1972. That is when I first saw it. I was thirteen. It was three weeks after my bar mitzvah. I was seeing it again 48 years later.

My father like, I suspect, many men of his generation, collected stamps. He did not buy stamps. He did not trade stamps. He did not go to stamp shows or correspond with other stamp collectors. He only collected stamps from envelopes he himself received in the mail. He was very fastidious about that. This, he believed, was how stamps should be collected. Our family and the few friends he had knew this, and would always send a letter, never a postcard, whenever they traveled abroad. He had a nice collection, and while most of the stamps were from Israel and Canada, he had stamps from an impressive list of countries. All teased from letters he had personally received in the mail.

He soaked the envelopes in a bowl of water, gently and delicately removed them with silver tweezers which had once belonged to his father, dried them on a red checkered terry cloth towel, then finally pressed them between volumes of the 1970 World Book Encyclopedia. I think it was letters N and M, as they were the heftiest. He then put them in a stamp album. The albums, they were olive green, were arranged chronologically. He had no categories. Did not separate by country. He entered the stamps as he received them. He would work on his stamps on Sunday mornings after a breakfast of ful (fava beans which are an Egyptian staple) and pita, hard boiled-eggs, and raw onions.

He collected stamps. That is just what he did. I never heard him talk about it. He never pulled out his albums to share with guests. I would sit with him on the kitchen table after my mother had cleared the remains of Egyptian days gone by. I did not eat *ful* in those days but Sunday was sweet cereal day - usually Cap'n Crunch, so I looked forward to it as much as my father did.

I don't remember having conversations with my father during those mornings. If we did, it would have been hard to hear because the Grundman record player would be blasting, well, blasting might be an exaggeration - Beethoven or Mozart, or Schubert. He knew all the music intimately and would sometimes close his eyes in bliss in anticipation of a passage. He would praise the piece, speaking words in French or sometimes, if the music really moved him, in Italian, and I would nod my head in agreement. No other words were exchanged. We just went along with our business and I would be given unspoken tasks.

He let me rip the corners off the envelopes, let me soak those corners in the bowl of water. He let me fold over the terrycloth towel and pat the stamps in an effort to speed up the drying process. He let me put the stamps in between the volumes of the encyclopedia, and I would look up at his face to see if today he would be ok with me sitting on the encyclopedia - depending on his mood - in order to really flatten the stamps. In time, he even let me enter the stamps into the album.

But he never let me touch the tweezers.

I don't think it was because he didn't trust me. I think it was because it was the task which gave him the most pleasure. He attacked it with surgical precision, angling a bedside lamp he carried into the kitchen just to have the best lighting. Truth is, most of the stamps quickly detached themselves from the envelope and ended up floating like lily pads in the bowl where they could easily be scooped up and laid out on the towel. But sometimes the stamp glue proved too stubborn and my father would pull out the tweezers. We both knew that another twenty minutes of soaking would probably do the trick but we also both knew it would deprive my father of the pleasure.

He would hold up the impeccably extracted stamp, hinges perfectly intact, and say "ah ha" as I stared wide-eyed. My bar mitzvah was coming up in a few weeks and, along with being called up to the Torah, I hoped a turn with the tweezers would be my rite of passage. The family was all abuzz about my bar mitzvah. For all the usual reasons but also because my father had invited Terry Humphreys.

Terry Humphreys was my father's boss. Somehow the subject of my bar mitzvah had come up in the lunchroom. Terry Humphreys said he had never been to a bar mitzvah. He was, he said, very interested in Jewish rituals. My father nodded his head and that is where it would have ended if my Uncle Henri, who had been quietly eating my Tante Nandi's *poulet soffrito* and *fasulia* out of a large red Tupperware, had not decided to pipe up and say, "You should come to the bar mitzvah." Which really left my father no choice.

I'm not sure what the French or Arabic equivalent of 'throwing someone under the bus' is, but it would have been pointless to say it in either because my Uncle Henri was convinced he had just done my father a huge favor. Either way, I had gone from the most nervous person in the Zevy family - I was reciting all the prayers, my *haftorah*, reading from the Torah, and had a speech to give to boot - to being a distant runner up.

At issue was who to sit Terry Humphreys and his wife, Clara, with. He would obviously be with my Uncle Henri and his wife, my Tante Nandi, but then who? Terry Humphreys and his wife Clara would be, aside from my friend Stevie Sheen, the only non-Jews. For a while, my father thought of inviting more colleagues from work and creating a Sherwin Williams table. But my mother convinced him the late invite would be in bad taste. In the end, he chose my Uncle Roger and Aunt Mira. Both were Egyptian Jews but Uncle Roger had grown up in England and had just a hint of an English accent. It was the best we could come up with.

In the end, it did not matter because Terry Humphreys had to cancel because he was going on a business trip to Malaysia. So, I went back to being the most nervous family member, had a bar mitzvah which went off more or less without a hitch, and did not think of Terry Humphreys until three weeks after my bar mitzvah when a very fat envelope, postmarked Malaysia, arrived in the mail. I tore into it and discovered a very nice note and 100 US dollars. It turns out that when Terry Humphreys asked my Uncle Henri what the appropriate bar mitzvah gift was Uncle Henri had replied "Cash is traditional." Which is not entirely true but he was doing me a solid. $100 was a shit-load of money in those days. Until then, the best gift I had received was a Sanyo cassette player from my Tante Racheline and Uncle Solly.

After much debate and discussion, my father agreed I would put 50 in the bank and could spend the other 50 - I had my eye on a mini pool table - on whatever I wanted. My father then handed me the envelope which had contained the magical hundred dollars and said "We don't have stamps from Malaysia." Little did we know that three years later we would be living on the Malaysian peninsula in the city-state of Singapore.

I only soaked the envelope for ten minutes. I knew what I was doing. I wanted to use those tweezers. But the stamp, the Malaysia twenty-five cent, was not ready to come off. I ripped it in two.

I had gone from elation to fighting off tears. Stamps were holy in our house. My father handled them like newborn babies. We could no more rip a stamp than we could rip a page from the Torah I had read from three weeks earlier. My father walked over from the sink where he had been scrubbing a pot and examined the damage. I braced myself for a stern lecture but it never came. "Those other two stamps are nice," he said, referring to the other Malaysian stamps which had been on the envelope. "Soak them for ten more minutes and we'll try again." But the stamps detached themselves in the water all by themselves and I never got to use those silver tweezers. Not that day and never again. I still sat with my father some Sundays and performed my tasks. But then I stopped - interests took me elsewhere. I think he may have stopped at some point too. I was much, much older before I realized it probably didn't have anything to do with collecting stamps after all.

I order the twenty-five-cent Malaysia from HipStamp for $3.25. It arrives four weeks later from a dealer in New Jersey. It takes me fifteen minutes to extract it from the cocoon where it has been safely ensconced.

It's nice. I look at it through my newly acquired magnifying glass. Nice. It is mint. Then I put it in my blue stamp album.

The stamps on the envelope from New Jersey are US 32 cents. They are of a soccer ball and a basketball. I already have four copies of those but I diligently tear the corner along with those of the other envelopes I received this morning and drop them into the popcorn bowl I use as a soaker.

The doorbell rings and it is my friend Downtown Darren Brown. We chat on the front porch for a while and by the time I get back into the house the stamps are already detached and doing the backstroke on top of the bowl.

I use my new silver tweezers to pluck them out of the water. I put the stamps in my olive green album.

# STRAIGHT SETS

Photograph © seoterra / 123rf.com

My Uncle Henri would not stop going on about Peter Raymond.

"Did you call Peter Raymond? Did you make an appointment with Peter Raymond? Why don't I see anything in your report about Peter Raymond?"

He had a bug up his ass about Peter Raymond.

Peter Raymond was the senior purchasing agent for Jackson Exhaust. Jackson Exhaust was a huge automotive parts manufacturer which used a clear powder coating to paint their exhausts. We made clear powder coatings. But Jackson Exhaust did not buy their clear powder coating from us. They bought it from Samson Paint—our biggest competitor.

My Uncle Henri did not understand why Jackson Exhaust did not buy clear powder coating from us.

"We have a beautiful clear," he said. If you closed your eyes, you would think you were listening to the late Egyptian President Anwar Sadat. If Sadat was the owner of a powder coating company and not the President of Egypt.

He was right of course.

We did make a beautiful clear powder coating.

But ours was not on the Jackson Exhaust automotive approval list.

Also, ours was about $1.00/kg more expensive.

Peter Raymond told me as much whenever he deemed to pick up the phone when I called him. He told me I was wasting my time. He told me they were very happy with Samson Paint.

But when I told my Uncle Henri these things, he looked at me as if I had just told him Yvan Cournoyer was not a fast skater. As if I had just told him his wife, my Tante Nandi, did not know how to cook.

"Ronnie," he lectured. "How many times have I told you. When they throw you out the front door, you sneak back in through the window."

I loved my Uncle Henri. But there is no way he ever snuck in through a window.

"I am coming to Toronto next week. I want you to make an appointment with Peter Raymond."


Peter Raymond would not take my calls. He would not return my messages. So I drove to Jackson Automotive and told reception I was here to see Peter Raymond. Did I have an appointment? I did not. "You should make an appointment." I tried to make an appointment. He won't return my calls. "You should make an appointment." I said, "Can you just tell him Ron Zevy of Protech Chemicals is here? I just need two minutes. I am happy to wait."

So I waited.

Six hours.

Three times Peter Raymond walked right by me, twice I presume on the way to the bathroom, and once on the way to an extended lunch with Mario Rossetti of Samson Paint.

Not once did he acknowledge my existence.

The receptionist smiled at me a few times. But I don't think she felt sorry for me. Nobody ever told me to go into powder paint sales.

Peter Raymond left his office door slightly ajar. I tilted my head just so I could see he was playing solitaire on his computer.

Red Queen on black King, you fucking piece of shit.

Finally at 4:55, the receptionist picked up her ringing phone and motioned me in.

I got straight to the point.

"My boss (I didn't say my Uncle) is coming into town. He wants five minutes to say hello. He knows you are happy with Samson Paint. He just wants to say hi."

"Sounds like a waste of five minutes," said Peter Raymond. I was going to tell him it was my job on the line but he agreed before I had to prostrate myself. But first he put the black 9 on the red 10.

Jesus, what an asshole.

Our appointment was at 10:00 am. Peter Raymond let us in at 11:55. My Uncle, God bless him, went to the bathroom three times while we waited.

"Your salesman here is quite persistent," said Peter Raymond.

My Uncle had a whole pitch ready for Peter Raymond. Five times he had repeated it to me in the car. How we had a better product. How we would provide better service. How cheap was going to cost them money in the long run. It was good. But I knew it wasn't going to work. But when we got into Peter Raymond's office, my Uncle Henri decided to call an audible.

This is what he said to Peter Raymond:

"You play tennis?"

I had no idea where he had come up with this, but then I saw the Donnay racquet, the one Björn Borg played with, propped up in the corner of the office. My Uncle had gone all Kevin Spacey in *The Usual Suspects* on us. He did that. He looked at family pictures. He looked at paintings on the wall. He looked for tennis racquets.

Peter Raymond reached over, grabbed the racquet and twirled it in his hand. He looked more like a majorette than a tennis player.

"Only in the summer," he said. "Too damn expensive to play indoors in the winter."

My Uncle Henri replied, "I know it is expensive." He pointed at me. "This one expenses it. I pay for it!"

He was right, I expensed my membership to Mayfair Country Club which had indoor courts.

Then my Uncle Henri threw me under the bus.

"I'm sure Ronnie would be happy to bring you to his club."

Then he shook Peter Raymond's hand and said goodbye.

Not a word about powder coatings.

Not a word.

When we got in the car, Uncle Henri decided to back up the bus and run me over a few more times.

"Are you a good tennis player?" He asked.

I said I was pretty good.

"Well," he said as he buckled up, "you have to let him win."


So for three months, every Wednesday night, I played tennis with Peter Raymond. Peter Raymond was shit. Every Wednesday, he beat me in straight sets. I would hit the ball long. I would hit the ball into the net. I would double fault. Peter Raymond beat me in straight sets every Wednesday. Then we would have a beer, to be fair, he had three, and he would give me tennis tips. I needed to bend my knees. I wasn't tossing the ball high enough.

I would write it into my report.

Played tennis with Peter Raymond.

Lost 6-3, 6-4.

My uncle was making another sales trip to Toronto. Could I set up another meeting with Peter Raymond? Peter Raymond said yes without batting an eye. Meeting was set for 10:00 am. He met us at 10:00 am.

"Henri, you've got yourself quite the salesman here," said Peter Raymond. "But maybe you should let him expense a few tennis lessons. I try giving him tips but he is really bad. And not getting better. He hasn't won a single set."

But my Uncle Henri did not want to talk about tennis. He wanted to talk about clear powder coating.

"Peter," he said slowly and carefully. "We would like a chance. Let us show you what we can do."

And then Peter Raymond shocked the hell out of me by saying, "Let's do a 10,000 kgs trial."

My Uncle Henri said, "Great."

Peter Raymond said, "Henri, these things take time. It isn't overnight."

Uncle Henri said, "We aren't in a rush. We are interested in a long-term relationship."

Peter Raymond said, "We know your paint. We have heard good things. It just has to pass the roof test."

I said, "Roof test?"

"Yes, we coat about 15 exhausts and put them on our roof for six months. We see how it deals with the sun and the elements."

Six months, I thought. Six months was a piece of cake. Our polyester clear could withstand six months in the sun standing on its head. Six months was nothing. I couldn't believe we were going to get the Jackson Exhaust account.

We all shook hands. Peter reconfirmed our Wednesday tennis match.

I knew better than to wait for praise from my Uncle, but I still fished for a compliment.

"10,000 kgs is a nice order," I said. "Sounds like they are serious."

My Uncle didn't say anything. I knew a compliment was a long shot. I didn't care. It was a nice order.

"I'll call the lab and tell them to send a sample for the roof test. Our polyester clear will have no problem passing. Six months is easy."

Then my Uncle said something which really surprised me:

"Don't bother."

I didn't understand. And I said so.

"We don't want to do business with these guys."

"Uncle Henri," I argued. "You have been bugging me about Jackson Exhaust for years. I have been playing tennis with Peter Raymond for three months and letting him win. We finally get an order and now you don't want to do business with them? I really don't understand."

My Uncle Henri turned to me. "You know anything about car exhausts?" It had to be a rhetorical question because he knew I didn't know anything about car exhausts. I told him no.

"When the car starts, it generates so much heat that the paint gets burned off the very first time."

I told him I didn't know that. "What do they need the paint for then?"

"It's just for display purposes. So it looks shiny and nice for the customer. When you go into," he struggled to remember the name of the car part store but then remembered, "like Napa Auto Parts."

I said I didn't understand. "Why would they want to test sun resistance by putting it on the roof for six months if it never gets exposed to the sun?"

"Because," he said as he popped one of my Tante Nandi's sambouseks into his mouth. "They are idiots."

"I agree. Peter Raymond is an idiot. But it is a pretty good order."

He wagged his finger at me.

"If there is one guy doing something dumb it means there is another guy letting him do something dumb. Who knows how many dumb people they have running the company."

I said, "Okay."

"Don't worry," he said. "There are other companies." Then he said something even more surprising than turning down a big order. "You didn't do a bad job."

I said thanks.

Then he said, "But it took you three years." But he was smiling when he said it.

Jackson Exhaust went out of business two years later. We heard they owed Samson Paint a lot of money. That's what we heard.

I only played tennis with Peter Raymond one more time.

I beat him in straight sets.

6-0, 6-0.

I guess his tennis tips paid off.

# SHESH BESH

I have a message from TorontoCityGirl44. She says "I love backgammon too."

I don't really understand what she means until I remember that backgammon is one of the hobbies listed on my profile.

Her profile has a lot of pictures of her hiking. One from Zion National Park in Utah. One from Sedona. And one from, Jesus, one from fucking Nepal. She is wearing one of those hats with the flaps that cover the ears. The ones Monty Python wear while singing the lumberjack song. The caption says "the altitude is giving me the best natural high."

TorontoCityGirl44 is not unattractive.

"We should play. Loser buys drinks." I may have used a happy face emoji.

"Be prepared to get crushed. I only drink champagne." Followed by a host of emojis I had never seen before. One may have been a waffle.

I take another look at her pictures and then 'like' her comment.

Dinner is on King Street. Far from my house but walking distance to her condo. It goes well. I make her laugh three times. I only engage the couple at the table next to us once. And this is only to insist they order the butternut squash soup instead of the gazpacho. Cold soup. Are we at war?

If interviewed, the couple would reveal that I displayed a genuine interest in Nepal. And perhaps a little too much interest in the hygiene habits of Sherpas. They are young. Youngish. He is wearing a sports jacket he may have only worn once before. They thank me for the soup suggestion. Make the requisite oohs and ahs. They both give me the thumbs-up. A real life emoji. But I feel they regret not ordering the gazpacho.

TorontoCityGirl44 goes to the bathroom. When she comes back, I notice she has reapplied her lipstick. I take it as a good sign. Later, when I tell the story to Ellen, she looks at me like I am an idiot. Reapplying lipstick is not a sign. It is just lipstick.

She does not fake-reach for her purse when the bill arrives. Which, to be honest, I appreciate.

"Are you ready to get your ass kicked?"

I smile and feign fear and apprehension.

The young man in the sports jacket once again gives me the thumbs-up. He has evaluated the situation, and based on his limited experience, determined that I was about to get laid.

I return the thumbs-up but do not share his optimism. If I had time I would explain it to him. But I don't. And anyway, it would take too long. He doesn't get it.

He doesn't understand.

Backgammon isn't just backgammon.

The smell is of burning meat. Kebabs and spicy merguez sausages. Cooking on a Hibachi grill. The charcoal, aided by kerosene starter, is now turning white. It has a salt and pepper look.

The music is Om Kalsoum. The famed Egyptian singer who, as legend is told, once took a Jewish lover. If it is Om Kalsoum, then we must be in my Uncle Henri's backyard. That is all he would ever play.

The other discernible sound is the crackling of the die as they rebound on the plain brown wood backgammon board. The French name for it—*tric trac*—best describes the sound. The die are tiny ivory cubes. Not the die we would later use for Monopoly or Snakes and Ladders. In Arabic, likely a derivative of the Turkish, it is called *Tawula*. But the most common name is *shesh besh*. The *shesh* comes from the Hebrew word for six and the *besh* is the Turkish word for five.

6-5.

That is a good opening roll.

The players are my Oncle Solly and Oncle Andre.

They are shirtless.

Shamelessly shirtless.

Watermelon juice running down their hairy chests as they take turns spitting the seeds across the backyard.

Oncle Solly was the coolest man I knew growing up. He drove a convertible Thunderbird and was a top guy at the Steinberg grocery store organization. He was charismatic and was an inveterate flirt.

The game was one of burgeoning testosterone. Insults, mostly in Arabic, some in French, flying as quickly as the pieces moved across the board. When they hit an unprotected piece, it was with a slam which could be heard at the Williamson house three doors down.

This was not a game. It was war.

Aggressive. Fearless. They played with what can only be described as unmitigated hubris.

The cousins, me amongst them, stood and watched. Sometimes asked to go fetch a beer or a piece of my Tante Nandi's baklava. We sometimes played on our own mini sets but mostly we watched.

Entranced.

Solly would play marathon sessions. I don't remember money-changing hands, but losses were not taken with grace. When the Uncles and older cousins would finally take a break in order to nap on the plastic lounge chairs, Solly would, with the twinkle in his eye, point to me and to the empty chair and say, "Ronnie, come show me how to play."

I tried to emulate what I had seen—minus the Arabic insults—but the game moved much too quickly. Hesitate for a second and Solly would move your pieces for you. Make the wrong move and his face would contort as if in pain. As if he had just been kicked in the balls.

"Ronnie Ronnie Ronnie," with a shake of the head and a wry smile.

Count the pips with your finger and there was a good chance Solly would reach over and try to snap it off.

Like my father would if we used our hands to gently push the scrambled eggs onto our fork. "We aren't animals," he would say.

Counting was for the Ashkenazim.

You needed to know the board. Needed to know every combination. Needed to know where every piece went with any and every combination of the die. Move to the wrong place and you would hear "non." First time gently. Second time not so much. Third time, well there hadn't better be a third time.

It's where I first saw the finger wag. A wag I would ultimately adopt as my own. When one of your pieces was off the board and your roll was one which had you blocked, Solly would hold up his big meaty hand and wag his index finger back and forth. No, my friend. You can't get in. Better luck next time. Those of you of a certain age will know the wag from the Babu character in Seinfeld.

You are a bad, bad, bad man, Jerry.

I hated that fucking finger.

And sometimes, the ultimate emasculation. When your roll afforded you only one possible move, he would make the move for you before the die even came to a full stop all the while shouting out "force" in French.

Forced.

The only move you were able to make. You were forced to make it.

With a big smile. A shrug of the shoulders.

It would be over quickly. Another cousin ready to take my place.

"Good game, Ronnie. I thought you had me. Bring me a cup of Turkish coffee. Tell your aunt not too sweet this time."

This is the shesh besh I grew up with. The shesh besh of Egyptian Jews. The shesh besh of Heliopolis. Of Alexandria. Of the Nile. Of the pyramids. Of the beach on Ras el Sum.

Aggressive.

Unrelenting.

It was a bloodsport.

It was not a game. We took it seriously. Of forced moves. Of finger wags. Of insults in Arabic. This was the only shesh besh I knew. This is the shesh besh I played.

It took me five minutes to know if you could play. Usually less.

And five minutes before I told you that you didn't know how to play.

This is the shesh besh I bring with me as I walk into TorontoCityGirl44's condo.

They say when you have a stroke you can smell burnt toast. I can smell Turkish coffee.

"Nervous?" She asks.

"No," I say as I wag Uncle Solly's finger. "Not at all. Why would I be nervous?"

# LOOKING FOR MAURICE

That is a picture of my mom, my sister, my Nona, my uncle Henri, and Tante Nandi, and Tante Joel circa 1970. I would have been 11. It is the living room of our house in Montreal. Look closely and you can see that uncle Henri, and both aunts, have cigarettes in their hands. An extra chair has been dragged from the kitchen so it must have been a party. A birthday maybe? I can see snowbanks out the window so that rules out my sister's or my May birthdays. My brother's is in March. Or maybe a Jewish holiday? Don't know. Doesn't matter.

I want you to focus instead on the painting above the sofa. It is a reproduction of a painting by turn-of-the-century French painter Maurice Utrillo.

I'm going to guess that none of you, even those with Art History degrees, will have heard of Maurice Utrillo. I am not being judgemental. There is no reason you would have. He was a second-tier, post-impressionist painter who specialized in scenes of the Paris neighborhood Montmartre. I don't know what this painting is called.

Not sure if you can really make it out. It is nice enough.

Now here's the thing about Utrillo. Even though he was considered a minor French painter, he still merited a paragraph in the 1970 World Book Encyclopedia.

The Encyclopedia was the internet before the internet.

Am sure there were many different types of encyclopedias. But really, there were only two that mattered: World Book Encyclopedia and Encyclopedia Britannica.

Before I continue, I need to talk about running shoes. In my day, and we don't need to get specific about what day that was, there were two choices for running shoes. Or, sneakers, should you be reading this south of the border.

The kids with money wore Adidas Rom—three stripes—the rest of us wore North Stars—two stripes.

That just about says it all.

Our world divided by how many stripes we had on our sneakers.

The World Book Encyclopedia was the two-stripe encyclopedia. Nevertheless, we had the entire collection, every letter, and it even included the 1970 year-in-review supplement.

And right there. Towards the end of the already slim volume for the letter *U*, was a paragraph about Maurice Utrillo.

I no longer have access to the 1970 World Book Encyclopedia, but I can Google him. Here is what Wikipedia, which, to be fair, is largely regarded as a two-stripe or, dare I say, one-stripe internet resource, says about Utrillo.

"Maurice Utrillo, born Maurice Valdon (1883-1955) was a French painter who specialized in cityscapes. Born in the Montmartre quarter of Paris, France, Utrillo is one of the few painters of Montmartre who were born there."

Here is what Artnet says:

"Maurice Utrillo was a French artist noted for his naive yet picturesque cityscapes. Rendered in thick troweled paint, the artist portrayed the winding streets and alleyways in the Montmartre neighborhood of Paris."

Am not sure what the World Book Encyclopedia said. I suspect it was somewhat prosaic and would not have said "naive yet picturesque." But still. Whatever it did say, it devoted an entire paragraph.

So, when I told friends we owned an original Utrillo, I had the World Book Encyclopedia to back me up. After all, who would doubt the authenticity of a painting by a painter they had never heard of? Not sure who the ten-year-old me was trying to impress. The rest of the house was two-stripe all the way. Still, it was my story and I was sticking to it.

We moved to Ottawa in around 1973. If the Utrillo came with us I really have no idea. If it hung on a wall, I don't remember. I have no pictures of our house in Ottawa save for one of the exterior. Utrillo, and his naive yet picturesque renderings, no longer figured in my life. Until university.

There is an art fair at the university commons the first week of school. They are selling prints for $5. Buried beneath one of the stacks of prints of French impressionists, I find an Utrillo.

*Sacre Couer en Hiver.*
Here is a picture of it.

I tape it up to the wall of my dorm room.

Is it a piece of home?

Don't get carried away. It is a print. I like it.

I'm only in the dorms for a year. My parents are back from Singapore. Does the Utrillo print make it to my bedroom? Side by side with who, Farrah Fawcett? No clue. No recollection. Do I bring it with me when I move to Toronto? Again. No clue. Unlikely.

That should end my Utrillo story, but I find myself in Paris one summer and visiting her famed museums is de rigeur. At the Orangerie, I come face to face with my first original Utrillo. I wonder how many more in the museum. I wonder how many more in the city. I look at my watch. It is still relatively early. I am in the city alone. I don't need anyone's approval for my plan: a day-long scavenger hunt trying to find as many Utrillos as I can. The Orangerie and Jeu de Paum are treasure troves, and I am able to pad my numbers from the get-go. But then I am adding ones and twos. I race through the Louvre with barely a sideway glance at the Mona Lisa and her throngs of Japanese tourists. I only have eyes for Maurice. I end the day with 22. I am alone and have nobody to high five but I am pretty pleased with myself.

I never repeat the scale of my scavenger hunt in subsequent visits, but I also never forget to look for Maurice whenever I am in Paris.

In 2009 I am in Israel for Passover and decide to make Paris my stopover on my way back to Toronto. My friend Carainn, her Irish background explains the unorthodox spelling of Karen, is on sabbatical, ostensibly, to learn French.

Carainn, though lovely and charming, does not have the gift of language. It has been three months and she has made no progress. I assume she has been skipping classes in order to go shopping but no, she assures me that she calls out "ici" every morning when attendance is taken. She does not seem the least bit perturbed by her lack of proficiency. She is loving the city and revels in showing me the sights.

The next day, Carainn is in class and I decide to go look for Maurice. I call the Musée de Montmartre and enquire about Utrillo. They have none. "The museum is closed today, Monsieur." And besides, don't I know there is an Utrillo and Suzanne Valadon (Utrillo's painter mother) exhibit at the Pinacotheque Museum?

This is what she says.
But what she means is:
Are you some kind of fucking moron?
I was.
And I am.

Carainn is a good sport. She is only too happy to go to the exhibit with me.

"How long is this going to take?"

This is Carainn being a good sport.

The Pinacotheque was an art gallery with exhibition space. It closed in 2016, but in 2009 it had the Utrillo/Valadon exhibit. Utrillo, it turns out, was an alcoholic who spent some time in an insane asylum. The exhibit was set up as a serpentine path with a start and finish. You couldn't wander around at your leisure. Nor could you really double back.

Anyway, it is a pretty cool exhibit and I kinda like that it has some structure. Carainn has rented the audio tour and, as a result, is spending a lot more time in front of each painting than I really care to.

And I do like the Utrillo. But all of it in one place is a bit overwhelming. It takes away from the charm of finding the occasional piece from time to time. He was my own personal two-stripe artist with only one paragraph in the World Book Encyclopedia, and now everyone knew about him. And Jesus, Carainn was taking so much damn time in front of each painting. I mean, it was cool. I was enjoying it. I think.

And then I turned the corner, and there it was. The painting from my living room. I looked for my family but I couldn't see them. Couldn't see anything through the tears in my eyes. Carainn caught up to me and began telling me the story about the insane asylum but stopped when she saw my face.

"Nice painting," she says.

"It's a good forgery," I reply, wiping away my tears. "My parents owned the original."

# CAESAR SALAD

I am down on the dock at the cottage with Danna and her friend Sally and they are trading blind date war stories. It really is a bit of a joke.

To begin with, 'blind' is such a misnomer that it is laughable. This generation has seen more pictures of their prospective dates than I have of my entire family collectively. When we went in blind, we really went in blind. Armed with no more, especially if the set up was from a female friend, than weathered adjectives about bubbly personalities and shared interests, and creatively ambitious promises about looks. "She looks a lot like Demi Moore," the wife might say while her husband bit his lip and stared downward at a fascinating piece of grass. I suspect tall tales were also told about me. I went on a lot of blind dates with women who, upon opening the front door, were completely unable to mask their disappointment. I saw a lot of the "Oh socks, I really needed socks" Christmas present look. A date most surely over before it had even begun, but now there would be two hours of forced conversation, "Do you like to travel? I love to travel", over plates of baked salmon and asparagus to look forward to. Then a perfunctory follow up phone call two days later in the quixotic hope that you completely misread the situation and that her look of only slightly contained nausea was in fact just one of concealed excitement.

These kids today have no clue. Nor any inkling of grammar or vocabulary. No need for a crack forensic team to decode a message on an answering machine.

Now they have emojis.

An emoji which takes care of sending a direct and unambiguous message about every situation. Should you be ambitious and take advantage of the richness of the English language, you might write 's'up.' Or, really dig deep into the well of words and type out a real tome - 'Netflix and chill.' Complete words and sentences are becoming rarer than a lunar eclipse.

"Now if I had access to text back in the day," I mused out loud.

I was not saying I could have done better. I was just saying I could not have done worse.

Danna's friend Sally, she actually does look a little like Demi Moore, asks if I have any blind date stories, and Danna rolls her eyes and says "He has a whole book of them." Which is true. I have written plenty of stories about blind dates.

"Tell the Caesar salad story," says Danna.

"It's a blind date story?" Asks Sally.

"Yes," chimes in Danna. "It is epic. Tell her who set you up."

I had forgotten about that. The phone number had come from my Tante Odette in Montreal. She called me every week for two months. I finally relented on week 9.

"Tonto," I say, referring to the nickname my family and all our friends call her.

"Tonto!" Says Sally who, having been friends with Danna since grade school, has an intimate knowledge of all of the members of our whacky family. "Oh, this is going to be good."

I get up and help myself to a couple of clementines from a bowl we have been sharing, cavalierly throwing the rinds into the trees behind us, assuming they are biodegradable. I return to my chair but not before first dragging it to a lonely square of shade I have found precariously close to the end of the dock

I toss a clementine to Sally. She and Danna, unlike me, have angled their lounge chairs in order to get the most of the late afternoon sun.

"Actually, the shocking part is that it was a good set up. Tonto played cards with a woman whose niece had just moved to Toronto."

"So you called her?"

"Yeah. But you have to understand it wasn't so straight forward. You had to find a good time to call and you couldn't just leave a message on the answering machine."

"Why not?"

"It just wasn't done. The first call had to be live. I think I hung up five times on the machine before I got through to her."

"That is jokes."

"No. What is jokes is she had never heard of me. She had no idea I was going to call. It took fifteen minutes before we could figure out the connection. I was surprised she even agreed to go out with me."

"Classic Tonto," says Danna.

"Why is it called the Caesar salad story?" Asks Sally.

I smile and answer.

"We went out for dinner and she ordered Caesar salad for an appetizer and Caesar salad with chicken as her main."

"Seriously?" Asks Sally.

"Yes," I reply.

"That's a true story?"

"Yup."

"That's a lot of garlic," says Sally. "Are you sure she wasn't trying to tell you something?"

"Maybe. But she went out with me twice more."

"The story gets better," pipes in Danna.

It is true. The story is much longer. But I don't like to tell it.

I suppose there are only so many stories but we writers always want to think we are coming up with something new and clever. Sometimes I choose not to tell a story, or at least not include it in a collection, because it seems a little too derivative. That is true of the Caesar salad story because the longer version is actually the 'the time I forgot my date's name' story and it sounds all too much like the classic Seinfeld 'Mulva' episode. I think it is a pretty good story and is really, beyond the forgetting of the name, really nothing like the 'Mulva' episode, but on occasion, when I tell it, someone will say "Oh, just like the Seinfeld episode," or worse, "Did you base that on the Seinfeld episode?"

And I don't really want to explain why it is different because the story is kind of ruined by then.

"This I gotta hear," says Sally.

So I tell the rest of the story.

Now I don't know how old I was when this happened but it doesn't really matter because there was never a time when I wasn't childish, immature, and juvenile and there was never a time when I didn't surround myself with friends who were also childish, immature and juvenile. And because we, Allie, Lewberg, Goldfarb, and I were childish, immature and juvenile, during the days between date one and date two and the days between date two and date three, we didn't call this woman by her given name.

Instead we called her Caesar salad.

As in "Where are you taking Caesar salad?"

Or:

"What time are you picking up Caesar salad?"

This woman, whose name will most assuredly come to me before I get to the end of this story, came to her nickname honestly. She ordered Caesar salad all three times we went out.

"Once at a Chinese restaurant," says Danna, stealing the thunder of my mid-story joke. It isn't true, of course. It is a fictional detail which found its way into the story and, as it does here, usually gets a big laugh and so earned its place in subsequent telling. It is a little unfair because, other than her unusual penchant for Caesar salad, she was funny, attractive, and very nice.

Date three was at the Dip on College Street. I didn't tell Lewberg, Goldfarb, or Allie where I was taking Caesar salad on our third date because I didn't put it past any of them to come snooping by, so it was likely a complete coincidence, although the patio at Cafe Diplomatico was one of my go-to places, when Lewberg suddenly appeared on College Street making his way to the corner of Clinton where she and I were sitting.

He was about fifteen feet away when I realized I had forgotten her actual name. We had used her nickname so often it had become lodged in my brain. Which sent me into an understandable panic.

When Lewberg got to our table, smiling at his good fortune for having discovered us, I looked up at him and said, mind you, to someone I had known for most of my adult life, "I'm terribly embarrassed but I have forgotten your name."

And Lewberg, unfazed or perhaps bolstered, by the number of Ketel and crans he had already consumed that night, had the good sense to stick out his hand and say "Lewberg. Nice to meet you."

Then she shook his hand and said "Sandra, so nice to meet you."

Then I said "Oh right, Lewberg. Of course, Lewberg. I am so sorry."

But what I meant to say was:

"Oh Right. Sandra. Sandra. Sandra. Not Caesar salad."

Then Lewberg, who is as solid a wing man as one could ask for, declined my offer to join us. Which may have been the one and only time he has ever turned down a drink.

"I love that part Uncle Ronnie," says Danna. "I have to give you credit. That was pretty smart."

"Yes," agrees Sally. "That was a baller move. Then what happened?"

"We went back to my apartment."

That's what we did. We went back to my apartment. I excused myself and went to the bathroom. I left Sandra in the living room where I had a fireplace. The fireplace had a wide mantle.

I don't keep that many pictures on my mantle. I have a few of my parents, my brother, my sister, my nephews and nieces. There is a picture of Sammy and I when I published No Nuts for Me. And a really nice group one from Pebble Beach from the time I got my hole in one.

Four of us.

The Pacific Ocean in the background.

Me.

Avram Kashitsky.

Goldfarb.

and Lewberg.

Lewberg.

That was the picture Sandra was holding in her hand when I came out of the bathroom in my apartment.

"Isn't that Lewberg?" She said.

"Omg!" Says Sally. "No way."

I say "Way."

"I guess you didn't go out with her again."

"Nope."

"Great story," she says. She gets up and heaves the clementine rinds into the trees then nudges the lounge chair with her knee in order to better greet the sun. My shade has shifted but I am too lazy to move my chair. Anyway, the sun feels good and the three of us soak it up without speaking.

And then Sally breaks the silence "You know," she says, "it kinda reminds me of that Seinfeld episode."

# I SHALL BE RELEASED

The Angel of Death is at my door. I start to shake. To his credit, he mollifies my fears right away. "No, no. I just need to use your bathroom. I have been on the job all night and haven't had a chance. I'm just bursting dude." I tell him be my guest. He rushes by me and makes a beeline for the bathroom.

I hear the water run. I guess the Angel of Death washes his hands.

He comes out wiping his hands on his trousers.

"A roll of paper towel wouldn't kill you. No pun intended. It's just good hygiene."

I tell the Angel of Death "My bad. I don't get many guests."

He says "It's all good. I see you read the New York Times. Interesting." I had read the Sunday Book Review on the toilet. I left it in the bathroom.

I say "The book review. Hoping they review something I have written one of these days." I don't know why I am telling the Angel of Death my hopes and dreams. I guess I am a little nervous.

He says "They won't print my letters to the editor. That Friedman doesn't have a clue." I don't know if he is just fucking with me.

The Angel of Death looks at his watch. He has a gold Rolex. He says "Listen, I've got a thing I need to do in about an hour. Do you think I can hang here?"

I say "Um."

"It's just I need to be close by. For this thing I need to do."

"In the building?" I ask. "You have a thing to do in this building?"

"I can't say. Just for," he checks his watch again, "57 minutes."

"Right, right. Sorry. I was just wondering. Of course you can stay. Can I get you a drink?"

"Do you have something peaty?"

I give him an 18-year-old Laphroaig. As I hand him the glass he says "Corner three bedroom".

I say "Really?"

He puts his finger to his lips and says "You didn't hear it from me."

The Angel of Death eyes the ivory chess set I have on my coffee table - it is really more decorative than anything.

"Game?" He suggests.

I look up and say "We have less than hour." The Angel of Death smiles and says "It won't take that long. Fischer was one of mine. Let's just say we took the long way home. He taught me a few things on the way."

The Angel of Death plays pawn to king 4. I make my move in reply.

"Sicilian Defence. Nice. This might take me a few more minutes than I thought."

I say "My father loved the Sicilian."

"Ah Marco," he says and my heart skips a beat. But before I can ask him anything, he spots my record collection and walks over to the shelf.

The Angel of Death now starts rifling through my record albums. He admires my turntable. "Old school eh? I haven't seen one of these in ages."

Old school eh? Is the Angel of Death Canadian?

"Yeah," I say. "I guess I am a bit of an audiophile."

The Angel of Death pulls out The Band's Music from Big Pink. "Oh man," he says. "Are you fucking kidding me. I love this. Can we put this on?"

I say "Be my guest. You don't get to listen to music where," I struggle to find the right words "where you come from?"

The Angel of Death gently places the vinyl on the turntable and ever so delicately lowers the needle.

"The old man has a thing for musicals," he says, not hiding his contempt. "I mean, I love Hamilton as much as the next guy but could you give me a break for the love of... well you know."

I say "Yeah," but I don't really.

We sit and listen to The Band. I help myself to my own pour of Laphroaig and top up the Angel of Death's glass. It gives me a chance to get a better look at him. He has the requisite goatee and a cowlick which looks like it is held down by gel. He is wearing khakis and a button-down shirt. If I didn't know he was the Angel of Death I would have guessed he was an assistant manager at Whole Foods.

I haven't listened to The Band for a long time too and the combination of music and scotch is creating a nice vibe.

We sing the chorus of *The Weight* together.

*"Take a load off Fanny*

*Take a load for free*

*Take a load off Fanny*

*And and, and… you put the load right on me"*

The Angel of Death has a nice voice. It is the last song on the first side. We sit in silence for a minute and then the Angel of Death starts chuckling.

"The old man was convinced it was Annie," he says. "Take a load off Annie. We had a huge fight about it. He almost had me go get Robbie Robertson to settle it. I had to talk him out of it. Talk about stubborn."

"Jesus," I say.

"Yeah. He put me on earthquakes for a year after that. Backbreaking work. I can tell you. He said it had nothing to do with it but you do the math." Then he flips the album and we listen to the other side.

When *I Shall Be Released* comes on the Angel of Death says:

"You know, I like this version better than Dylan's."

I say "I do too."

And then the Angel of Death says "Levon Helm. So fucking great." The Angel of Death might be a little drunk.

I say "Yeah, so fucking great." I might be drunk too.

"Hey, I am going to take another whiz and be on my way."

I say "Let me grab you a paper towel."

"Thanks man."

The Angel of Death comes out of the bathroom singing "Any day now, any day now, I shall be released," smiles, then says "Thanks for the hang."

I say "My pleasure."

He says "I understand if you say no but any chance I can take the album. I am going to try and sneak it in."

I take the record off the turntable, slip it back into the sleeve and hand it to the him. A CD might be easier to hide but I am not about to argue with the Angel of Death. We say our goodbyes. I put the scotch glasses in the dishwasher.

Twenty minutes later I hear a knock

The Angel of Death is at my door.

"You going to the Greenberg wedding next week?"

I say "Yeah."

And he says "You might want to take an Uber."

# SPEAKING ARABIC

Photograph © Around Egypt Tours

So I am having dinner at Tutto Pronto with my friend Ellen. We have arrived early and are waiting for the rest of our party to arrive. Ellen is having a glass of cabernet and I am drinking a Stella. There is a couple at the table next to us and the woman is giving the waitress a bit of a hard time with her order. Ellen and I don't even pretend not to notice the drama unfolding next door. The woman wants salmon but is very particular about how she wants it cooked. She is also not happy with the choice of vegetables and wants to know what the other options are. The waitress patiently and diligently lists the other possible choices and the woman wrinkles her nose at each one.

Ellen takes a sip of her wine, leans over, and whispers, "Hohtnah."

I should tell you Ellen is an Ashkenazi Jew. The only daughter of a Holocaust survivor father who was from Poland. By all rights, the snide remark she is making should be in Yiddish. Yiddish is an extremely colorful language and many of its words have permeated the English language lexicon and North American culture in large part because of television and film. There is a long list of Yiddish words she could have chosen to describe the woman's actions. Instead she has chosen a word in Arabic.

Arabic is spoken by over 400 million people in the world. But for the better part of my childhood the only people I knew who spoke Arabic were Jews.

Egyptian Jews.

My parents, my aunts and uncles, and their friends. All Egyptian Jews.

Arabic was my Yiddish.

And, just like Yiddish, the words were used as standalones (shmuck!) or, more often, tagged onto a sentence (you are such a putz) otherwise only containing words in French.

"*Je vous souhait milles mabruks.*" I wish you a thousand congratulations.

Every word in French other than the Arabic word for congratulations.

"*Va faire sortir la zaballa.*" Go take out the garbage. I have written before how both my brother and I grew up thinking *zaballa* was a word in French.

So we didn't know how to speak Arabic. But we knew a lot of words.

And our parents, aunts and uncles, took great delight in hearing the children and grandchildren utter those words, words we would not dare say out loud in French and English, back to them. When my Tante Odette does or says something a little wacky, I tell her she is magnoun—crazy. Every single time she laughs uproariously. Try telling your own aunt she is crazy and see what happens. My niece Danna has taken the word and put her own millennial spin on it. "Oh my god, she is so 'maggie!'"

But our favorite is hohtnah.

Hohtnah.

Leave me alone. Stop being such a pain in the ass. It was spat out, half in jest, half in spite. Sometimes whispered under one's breath right in front of the guilty party.

Hohtnah.

Ellen and I have been friends for a long time and it has entered our vernacular. She is using it here in part as a tip of the hat to me and my Egyptian Jewish heritage but mostly because Ellen loves words. And "hohtnah" is a great word.

It is a great word not only because of how it is used and why it is used. But it is a great word because of what it means.

Because the literal translation is a great example of the poetic beauty of Arabic.

Because literally, "hohtnah" means enema.

And if that's not a pain in the ass, then I don't know what is.

# KASHKAVAL

Rabbi Jose the Galilean did not look happy. It was the morning before the first night of Passover and I was in Ararat, the Armenian deli a few blocks from my house, in order to pick up a slab of Bulgarian kashkaval cheese, some kalamata olives, and a jar of blackberry jam from Georgia. The Georgia with the hard to pronounce capital of Tbilisi.

Passover, the week-long holiday celebrating the Jewish exodus from slavery in Egypt, was the most observed of all of the Jewish holidays. More even than the High Holy Days of Rosh Hashanah and Yom Kippur. Secular Jews who, during the year added sizzling bacon to their scrambled eggs and always included pork spare ribs to their Sunday night Chinese food orders were now ridding their houses of any sign or remnants of bread and schlepping up their Passover dishes from the basement. It was a strange and confounding phenomenon and one I could never get my head around. To truly understand Jews and Judaism, one need first understand the existence of kosher-for-Passover toothpaste.

I did not adhere to strict Passover dietary laws. Truth be told, I did not even adhere to lax Passover dietary laws. But I had adopted a Passover tradition of having a nice piece of buttered matza along with a chunk of kashkaval for breakfast. It was a tradition passed on from my grandfather to my father, from my father to me, and one I would gladly pass on to my own children should I ever make it past a second date.

And so I had stopped at Ararat in order to pick up the cheese and who did I run into but Rabbi Jose the Galilean. He was dressed, as was his custom, in black, with a grey beard which nearly ran to the floor.

He lived in the neighbourhood and I would often see him in Ararat where he would like to buy a small piece of halva, the Rabbi had a sweet tooth, drink a cup of Armenian, woe be the person who mistakenly called it Turkish, coffee and chat at the counter about the meaning of life with Mr Zakarian, the shop's jovial and portly owner. It is at the counter where I saw him. He did not, as I said, look very happy.

"Hi Rav," I said, greeting him with the honourific title which he had long earned and deserved "Hag kasher and sameach."

Rabbi Jose the Galilean did not have much reason to be happy. He had married a younger woman who turned out to be a terrible shrew. One who spent all day making fun of him in front of his very own rabbinical students and gave him nothing but tsores. He could not divorce her because she had come with a large dowry he was unable to pay back. His students, finally taking pity on their esteemed rav, raised the money to free him from bondage. The divorce, you would have thought, should have brought Rabbi Jose the Galilean some measure of happiness but alas, it was not to be. His ex-wife had married the town watchman who, as bad luck would have it, became blind and could not watch over anything, much less the town. Jobless, the watchman and his shrew of a new wife, hey I'm just repeating what I heard, had to resort to begging for alms. They finally, reluctantly, because although she might have been a shrew she was not without pride, found themselves in front of Rabbi Jose the Galilean's house. The Rabbi, although having questionable taste in women, was pious and generous, and he ended up taking in his ex-wife and now blind husband. They were now living with him. So he had plenty of reason to be unhappy.

But that wasn't why he did not look happy.

He wasn't happy because of me.

Not wishing me chag sameach in return, he must have been really angry, he said "I heard you have been skipping my section in the Haggadah."

Fucking Lewberg!

That very morning I had told Lewberg that the year prior I had finally convinced my brother and his family to skip over pages 18 and 19. It was a section which was nothing other than commentary by a group of rabbis discussing how many actual plagues the Egyptians had encountered at the Red Sea. It did not, I had argued, add anything to the story, was completely irrelevant and superfluous and, most of all, kept us precious minutes further away from Bubby Judy's pickled brisket. I thought I had made a salient and convincing argument and my family decided, I suspect just to shut me up, to skip over that section with the Rabbis.

The problem was that one of those Rabbis was now standing right in front of me.

"Lewberg?" I asked. I knew it was Lewberg. Who else could it be. The Rabbi liked to bet March Madness and Lewberg would help him lay down his bets.

Rabbi Jose the Galilean shrugged his shoulders and for the briefest of moments the anger dissipated from his body "Those schmucks were giving me Oral Roberts and laying 11.5 points. It was like taking candy from a baby."

"Rav," I said "I'm so sorry. It's just that the seder is so long and that pickled brisket is so good."

"How could you skip my section?" he said. And with that, he stormed out of the store.

At the very same time, my phone vibrated. It was a text from Lewberg.

It said "I think I might have fucked up."

I eat bread on Passover, I do not fast on Yom Kippur, I drive a car and light a fire on shabbat, and I have, more than once, coveted my neighbour's wife. Not my next door neighbour mind you, but a couple who live three blocks down. But you get the drift. I'm not the best of Jews. But of all of the transgressions I have committed, none made me feel worse than the way I threw shade on Rabbi Jose the Galilean.

I called Lewberg and, now being a little angry myself, did not even give him time to apologize.

"Dude," I said "forget about it. What's done is done. Just give me the Rav's address."

"I will text it to you."

Then I said "Oral Roberts?"

"11.5 points," he replied, "I think it is a no brainer."

"Ok, put me down for $100."

Then I went to buy some expensive kosher for passover chocolate and find the rabbi.

Let me say that Rabbi Jose the Galilean's ex-wife was not a shrew. Or, if she was, she was certainly not a shrew to me. She served me very good coffee and macaroons. I'm not so crazy about those macaroons. But still. Then she further ingratiated herself to me by saying. "I read your stories to my husband. They are so amusing."

And her husband, who I had not seen sitting on a rocker in a darkened corner of the room piped up "That Goldfarb is quite a character!"

Then Rabbi Jose the Galilean, a feather duster in his hand, still cleansing his house of the evil hometz, walked into the living room. I leapt to my feet, spilling some of the coffee, and began to launch into my apology. But I was not able to get a word in.

"Aaron Aaron Aaron Aaron," he said, invoking my given Hebrew name which only my father and publisher ever used "I cannot wait for Yom Kippur in order to ask for your forgiveness. I was so small and petty. And to not wish a fellow Jew a kasher pesach- it is a shonda. Please accept my apology."

"Rabbi Rabbi Rabbi," I replied "it is me who should be apologizing to you. I will make sure we recite that section in both Hebrew and English tonight."

"Ach," he said, waving me off with one hand and helping himself to a macaroon with another. "It is a stupid section. I know the Torah and Mishnah backwards and forwards. It is like the air I breathe. I have argued, successfully I might add, with Akiva, Tarfon, and Eliazar. And this is the only thing I am known for. Bah. The number of plagues. It is such a trifle."

"Yes," I said "it is a shame."

"By the way," he added "The number is fifty. Fifty plagues. Don't let anyone tell you different."

"Ok," I said.

"Do you know that Galilean is a term of derision? It is meant to denote a country, how do you say, bumpkin, a fool."

"You are a great sage Rav. After all, it was you who said you could have milk with chicken."

"Ah, so you know that. You surprise me young Aaron."

"Well, I did a little bit of reading. I think you were right."

"What can I tell you. The others were so rigid. So inflexible. But those are matters for another day. We still have to prepare for Pesach. So go Aaron. Go have a chag which is kasher and sameach."

"You too," I said. "By the way, I put $100 on Oral Roberts."

Then Rabbi Jose the Galilean smiled. I think it was the first time I had ever seen him smile.

He said "It's a lock."

Our 7:30 seder did not start until 9:00. We were all hungry and some a little cranky. So my suggestion that we now read pages 18 and 19 was met with a chorus of boos.

"Wait wait wait," I shouted over the tumult. "Here's what I propose. This year we put back the two pages of Rabbi Jose the Galilean but remove the three pages which are commentary from Rabbi Gamliel. It is a net win."

My nieces all flicked through their copies of the Haggadah.

"It's true," said Danna. "Gamliel has more pages. We can skip him and put back Jose the Galilean."

"That's what you want?" Asked my brother, who had long tired of arguing with me.

"I mean," I said, "do we really want the kids to grow up not knowing exactly how many plagues were inflicted on the Egyptians at the Red Sea?"

"You understand how you always get your way?" Said Caroline with a laugh.

"I do. And I appreciate it."

"And what do we get in return?" Asked my brother.

"Well, I did bring you some very good kashkaval," I said. My brother shared in the family tradition.

"Ok," he said. We will blow off Rabbi Gamliel. But it's on you."

That was fine. Rabbi Gamliel lived clear across town and I was unlikely to run into him.

And also, he didn't bet on basketball.

# THE KOTEL

Photograph © Moshe / Lakewood Fogels

When Harold heard I was going to Israel to visit my sister, he asked if I could bring something for him. Now Harold and I have been friends for a long time, and he is well-aware of my no-shlepping rule, so I knew he wasn't going to saddle me with a big package. Truth be told, I knew he wasn't going to saddle me with any package at all. So I was pretty confident when I walked into his house. My confidence was not unfounded, because he directed me to a small folded piece of paper which lay on the kitchen table. I immediately knew what it was for, and I quickly told him I didn't think I would be going to Jerusalem this time.

He said, "Take it just in case."

I said, "Okay."

My brother, sister-in-law, and youngest niece, Rena, were going to Israel in order to visit my sister and her family.

My sister lives in the town of Ramat Beit Shemesh. It is an Anglo-Orthodox town located almost midway between Tel Aviv and Jerusalem. I say Anglo because most of the inhabitants are former Americans, Canadians, Brits, and South Africans. There are native-born Israelis, but it is predominantly families who immigrated to Israel—made aliyah—from elsewhere. Many, not all, are also former secular Jews who then became more religious later in their lives. My sister and brother-in-law fit into that category. It is said one can gauge the type of Jew you are by your choice of head covering. My brother-in-law and his sons and sons-in-law all wear black hats. They are strictly kosher and pray three times a day.

I don't cover my head and enjoy the occasional cheeseburger.

But despite our differences, we are a very close family.

We were staying at a hotel in Tel Aviv and the plan was to split up our time between the beach and visiting our family.

We arrived on a Tuesday and we all dined together on Wednesday night, on Thursday night, and then spent the entire Sabbath at their house in Ramat Beit Shemesh. Friday night dinner. Saturday lunch. Saturday dinner.

It was fantastic!

My sister is a great cook and hanging out with my nephews, nieces, and their respective babies was a real treat.

My sister is an actual bonafide matchmaker and has quite the reputation in her town. Neighbours dropped by all day in order to greet the 'brothers from America.'

Let me say it again—it was fantastic!

But, much like the famed scene in *Blazing Saddles*, by the end of the day on Saturday, the sun couldn't set fast enough for us.

We said our goodbyes and took a taxi back to our hotel in Tel Aviv.

Sunday was a pool and beach day. We rented bikes and ambled down the 'Tayelet,' the Tel Aviv beach promenade. We texted with my sister and the kids during the day but mostly just to touch base.

We ended the day on the beach with olives and hummus and a cold Israeli beer.

Rena asked if we were going to see the family that night, but it looked like we would have a night alone. We really didn't feel like going back to Ramat Beit Shemesh.

We threw out the idea of meeting in Tel Aviv for dinner, but although Tel Aviv was but 40 minutes away, my sister had only been five times in 15 years.

"Why would I go to Tel Aviv?" she would say. I knew what she meant. Tel Aviv was the center of secular non-religious life in Israel. It was easier to find a kosher restaurant in Toronto.

So we knew our offer was akin to a Yom Kippur lunch invitation.

But then my brother and I began to feel guilty.

"If you want, we'll meet you in Jerusalem for dinner."

It was 8:00, we hadn't showered, and Jerusalem was an hour away.

Now you have to understand. Three of the kids had babies. My sister didn't like to leave the house at the best of times. Only one of them even had a car.

So, it was mostly just a bluff.

My niece Shoshanah was the first to call the bluff.

She texted, "The Marcuses are in! We will take the train."

Then Ariel said, "Okay, Jerusalem sounds fun."

Then Natan said, "Us too. We might be a little late."

Then Ben, Ben who had two babies who already should have been in bed, who was careful and deliberate, said, "We just ordered a taxi."

Now although my sister is loath to leave the house, certainly at this hour, she is stricken by a greater affliction.

FOMO.

Fear of missing out.

So her text, "We're also on our way," did not come as a surprise.

Rena was thrilled. My sister-in-law, to her credit, was a real sport. "It will be an adventure," she said.

We jumped in a taxi of our own and made our way to Jerusalem.

It was a little after 10:00 when we made it to Mamilla Mall—the shopping and restaurant mall just outside the gates of the Old City.

Fearing we might not get a taxi to get home, I threw down some bills and asked our driver if he wouldn't might waiting. I said we wouldn't be long.

We were a big group. We sent out a team to try to secure a table for 12. The Italian restaurant seemed perfect, but Ben wanted to first talk to their kashrut supervisor to make sure it was at their level of kosher. My brother gives me a look. He is going to faint from hunger. Luckily my brother-in-law arrives and gives the thumbs-up. We can eat here.

Our waitress is Tali. My sister begins to pepper her with questions. "What does it come with?" "Can I substitute this?" My brother bangs his head on the table. I decide to take over. I order multiple pizzas, pastas, and salads. I over-order.

"Ronnie, that is way too much," argues my sister.

"Who will take leftovers home?" I ask.

Everyone raises their hands.

Dinner is great, but it is now midnight. I am worried about the taxi driver. I dial the number, but Natan takes my phone.

"Achi—my brother—" he says. "This is Gingi—he uses the Hebrew term for redhead—we are going to be a little late. Beseder? Okay?"

The taxi driver says, "Eyn bayot. No problem."

We are too full for dessert. Leftovers are being packaged. Babies being once again rocked to sleep. It was a bonus dinner manufactured from whole cloth. You can say what you want, but you just can't beat family.

It is late. We are exhausted. We still have an hour ride back to Tel Aviv. But it was worth it.

We begin to say our goodbyes, and then my sister shocks the hell out of me by saying, "We have to go to the Kotel." The Wailing Wall. The Western Wall. It is the holiest and most revered place in all of Judaism.

I say, "What?"

My sister calmly says, "You can't go to Jerusalem without going to the Kotel."

I say, "It is 12:30 am."

But Rena says, "She's kinda right, Uncle Ronnie. You can't go to Jerusalem without going to the Kotel."

Everyone agrees.

I hand the phone to Natan.

He calls the taxi driver.

"Achi," he says, "it is Gingi. Tishma, listen, we are going to the Kotel." They are now talking like old friends. The taxi driver says he isn't going anywhere.

So the 12 of us, pushing baby carriages through the narrow cobblestone streets of the Armenian Quarter, make our way to the Kotel.

We turn the corner, past the old ladies selling red thread to ward off the evil eye, and there it is.

The Kotel.

And the courtyard is packed. It is teeming with people.

Black hats.

Knit kippas.

Baseball caps.

No hats.

Everyone goes to say a prayer.

I am not religious.

I don't pray.

But now I remember my friend Harold has given me a note to slip in between the cracks in the wall. The Jewish equivalent of throwing coins into Trevi Fountain. I had forgotten about it, and between seeing my family and being in Tel Aviv, we hadn't been to Jerusalem. I push my way through the throngs of men who are swaying back and forth in deep prayer and find myself in front of the wall. This ancient wall which was said to have been some part of the old temple. I pull out my wallet and find the note. The cracks in front of me are already full of notes. I don't know what becomes of them. I guess they get gathered every morning and sent to some rabbis. I really don't know.

Anyway, I don't really want Harold's note to get mixed up with the others. He has MS. He is in a wheelchair. I mean, I don't really believe in this stuff, but I am here. My sister's stubbornness has put me right here.

I see a crack, but it is out of my reach. I turn to two black-hat-cladded men, really just boys, praying next to me. One catches my eye and I point to the crack. I try to formulate a request in Hebrew in my head but I don't have to. Within five seconds, I am given a boost. Like the boost I used to get to sneak over the wall into the public pool back in Montreal. I slip in the note and start to thank the boosters but they have resumed their prayers.

My family regroups.

I say, "Can we go now?"

My sister says, "Now we can go."

The taxi driver and Natan hug.

We all want to sleep in the car, but the taxi driver announces he has cataracts. He doesn't usually drive at night.

I volunteer to stay up and guide him back to Tel Aviv.

Truth is, I am no longer all that tired. I am a little wired. I might have a touch of Jerusalem Fever.

Shoshanah texts the next day, "Thanks, Uncle Ronnie and Uncle Dov. Best night ever!"

She is not wrong.

Back in Toronto, I invite myself for lunch at Harold's house. They have hummus and olives. I tell him I delivered his note. I tell him I slipped it into one of the higher cracks.

"Closer to God," he says. But I know he is mocking me.

"So what was in the note?" I ask. "Or is it like a birthday wish?"

He is smiling now. His wife, Gili, is laughing.

I wait. And then he tells me.

"The note was blank. I just wanted to get you to the Kotel."

# PHOTOGRAPHS

Photograph © Elena / 123rf.com

This story is nominally about an old photo album I found containing pictures from a trip my parents took to Spain many years ago. I should tell you in advance the story involves pictures of topless women at a beach. If that sort of thing offends you, you should probably stop reading. The album is one of ten we retrieved from my mother's condo when she passed away. We took the photo albums and put them in suitcases which then went into my garage along with her black leather couch and a handful of paintings which my parents brought back with them from Singapore. We were going to get to them but we never did. My nieces called their respective dibs on the couch and paintings but they never moved either. I guess they were taking a futures option. Then, one day, I knocked down the garage in order to build a deck (full disclosure: I knocked down the garage in order to build a golf simulator, but logic, pragmatism and local zoning laws stopped that in its tracks), and all the contents were moved to an outside shed.

This spring, I decided to replace the dilapidated shed and, in doing so, rediscovered the two suitcases containing the ten photo albums from my mother's condo. I dragged the suitcases into my basement and quickly discovered the shed and suitcases were not exactly Timex-watch-waterproof, so I had to dry out some of the photos and went to a photo editing store which specializes in restoring water-damaged pictures.

A week before my father passed away, I wheeled him down to the garden in front of his Toronto condo in order to take advantage of a nice spring day. He had already stopped reading by then. He told me, in not so many words, that he had had a good run. Marriage, family, friends, Florida, career, books. He was being philosophical but not in the least bit bitter. I asked him if there were things he had still wanted to do and he surprised me by saying travel. We had lived three years in Singapore and literally gone around the world. He planned his trips meticulously and nothing gave him more pleasure than spreading out a map on the kitchen table and planning out our destinations. The photo albums contained both pictures of our family trips and those he and my mom had taken with friends. This specific album was dated 1986, and it was of a trip they took to Spain with their best friends Taki and Anna Kizas.

In 1986, I was 27 years old and already living in Toronto while my parents were still in Ottawa. I don't remember anything about their trip. No stories. No anecdotes. Taki was a colleague of my father's from work. Though Greek Catholics, the Kizas family story was very similar to the Zevys. I'm quite certain they had actually grown up in Alexandria and so had the Egyptian connection.

When my father passed away, rather than follow the traditional Jewish mourning rules and rituals, I chose to honor and memorialize him by reading some of the books in his heady collection. I thought it to be a fitting tribute although not necessarily one he might have been on board with. When my mom passed away, I took possession of her two prized address and phone books—one for Canada and one for Florida—and endeavoured to call people in her life which were part of her regular and disciplined phone schedule. She would flip through her book and decide who to call and regale with the latest exploits of her beloved grandchildren.  Now I was making some of these calls. They were not always easy. There were distant cousins whose only link to our family was via my mom. "Ronnie," I would yell on the phone. "Le fis de Nanda." (Nanda, short for Fernanda, was my mom's nickname for most of the Egyptians.) "Ah," they would reply, finally understanding, "the unmarried one." "Yes, yes, the unmarried one." Anna Kizas was on my regular call list. No woman, before or since, has ever been as happy to hear from me. My Tante Regine is a close second, but Anna always made the top of the list because she promised to pray for me in church. I'm not a religious man, but if I wanted someone to pray for me, it would be Anna Kizas. Her and Taki were two of the nicest and finest people you could ever hope to meet.

The Spain album is devoted entirely to their trip. It is not, like some of the other albums, a mish-mash of different trips and people. It was what you would expect in terms of pictures from two middle-aged couples vacationing in Spain. Cafes and vistas and churches and beaches and bulls (not really any bulls) and cobblestone streets.

Plus nine photos of topless women.

These are not pictures of the beach which happen to have topless women lying in the background. These are pictures taken specifically of topless women.

They were not in some hidden compartment or folder in the photo album. And yet, this was the first time, all these years later, I noticed them. Again, let me reiterate, this is not one photo lost amongst a sea of others. This is not *Where's Waldo*. Nine photos. And I had never noticed them before.

I can hear Ellen saying, "That's because they aren't pictures of you, Ron." I think that is a cheap shot. Sure, maybe I might have ignored pictures of random cousins, but this made no sense.

Now, the last thing I want to do is disparage Taki and Anna Kizas, but there is absolutely no way Marco Zevy took these pictures. My mother, may she rest in peace, did not know how to operate a camera.

But here's the thing.

Maybe these pictures did come from Anna and Taki's camera. They took them to the local photo development store. I am going to say Black's camera on Bank Street. The girl behind the counter would have said, "Do you want two sets?" Before Taki or Anna, or maybe their son Johnny or daughter Mary sent to run the errand, could answer, because she did this 25 times a day, she would say, "Second set is only an extra $1." Taki, or Anna or Mary or Johnny would say, "Okay, why not."

Taki would then call my dad and say, "Marc," not Marco, "the pictures are ready." When could he drop them off? My mother would surely invite him in for Turkish coffee and a kaak or sambusek or malmul. Would they then look through them, sitting on the rattan couch my parents had brought back from Singapore? Will you look at that! It is, to borrow the words of Wallace Shawn in *The Princess Bride*, inconceivable. In my life, I never heard my father make a sexual comment about a woman. Maybe, maybe, one time in the Tivoli Gardens in Copenhagen, he might have said something about the high percentage of beautiful women. But that, in my mind, would have been a math-related comment.

And then what? My father would not have dilly-dallied. It was not his style. He would have placed the photos in the album right away. Maybe he waited until Sunday. The photo album, with its sticky back and transparent flap for each page. And he would have carefully and meticulously laid out the pictures. Including all nine pictures of the topless women. Were the pictures laid out in some sort of chronological order? Was there more than one beach?

When I was young, I babysat at the next-door neighbors. I don't remember their name or that of the kids. They were very nice people who paid me generously. Their living room coffee table was one which had a cubby below the surface where they stored magazines. One of the magazines was *Playboy*. Right there almost in the open. We did not have *Playboy* in our house. I also could see, but never touch, the *Playboy* magazine at the barber. "Don't tip him, he is the owner," my father would say. Words I no longer live by. I never looked at the *Playboy*. Nor did my father. He read *The Story of Civilization* by Will and Ariel Durant.

I don't want to suggest my father was not a man. But, he was not, to me at least, that kind of man. Not the kind of man who I read about in memoirs who takes their kid to a whorehouse on their 18th birthday. The only conversation we ever had about sex, and it wasn't really even a conversation at all, was the summer of my 17th year before a backpacking and youth hostel trip to Europe. One of the destinations was to be Amsterdam. "There will be women behind windows," he said. I nodded my head okay. "Do you understand?" I said I did but I didn't. "Don't go inside." I said okay. And that was it. I later saw the women. I didn't go inside.

I bring the photo album with me to the cottage. I show it to my brother, my sister-in-law, and to my nieces. I show it without describing the contents.

"Why are there all these pictures of topless woman?" asks Rachel.

My sister-in-law's parents are at the cottage. Although not quite my parents' generation, they are of a generation. They are the least shocked of all of us. "We all took those pictures," says Judy. "Every North American who went to a beach in Europe came back with pictures of topless women. It was like taking pictures of zebras on an African safari." It was part of the wild life. "But I can tell you something for sure. Your father didn't take those pictures though," she said authoritatively. "Nor did he put them in the album. That was your mother." Everyone nodded their heads. Yes, they agree, this had Nona's handiwork all over it.

So that was that.

Mystery solved.

But I am not convinced.

"Hand me that album," I say. "Let me look at those pictures one more time."

# ABDULLAH THE BUTCHER COMES FOR LUNCH

My best friend growing up was Stevie Sheen. Our backyards, in the Montreal suburb of Dollard des Ormeaux, were connected, and since there was no fence to separate the two properties, it created a double-sized space where we could throw the ball around for hours and then play Stratomatic baseball until our moms called us in for our respective dinners.

And while Stevie Sheen was my best friend; I was not his. That honour would fall to Mike Leese. Now Mike was not only a year older than us and a year ahead in school, but he was a much-heralded multi-sport athlete. The parents, the Sheens and the Leeses, were good friends. My parents had no friends who had not been born in Egypt. Quite honestly, it was hard to begrudge Stevie for picking Mike. It was, by any account, quite a score. And also, not to nitpick or be overly sensitive, but he was a best friend in name alone. If Stevie had to fill out a form which said "In case of emergency who is your best friend?" then he would put down Mike Leese, but the facts on the ground, which were all that I cared about, told the real story.

Anyway, as I said I didn't begrudge him. I actually quite liked Mike Leese, and the fact that he hung around with Stevie meant that I, a friend by association, got to hang around too. It was a perfectly good arrangement and did not adversely affect my life, other than the fact that Mike Leese and I shared the same birthday. And so, in our family albums, there are no pictures of Stevie Sheen having birthday cake with me, because he was having birthday cake with Mike Leese's family and friends.

It never really bothered me, but my mother, may she rest in peace, could never really get her head around why the shaggy-headed gentile from the backyard who felt comfortable enough to track mud on her kitchen floor never showed up for her sambousak, konafa, and two layered chocolate cake.

"Stevie vien cet année? Is Stevie coming this year?" She would ask. And I would shake my head no. She would shake her head back in disappointment. I think she felt bad for me, and nothing I would say could dissuade her from thinking that. Even my father, the mathematician, coming to my side to say that 364/365 was a pretty good result, did not assuage her.

That's only to say that when I told the lie, the lie which is this story, I was mostly thinking about my mother and not about me.

Mendel Good passed away last year. He was 95. Mendel was a Holocaust survivor. His tale of his escape from the camps would make the hairs on your arms stand on their proverbial ends. He had seen things and lived things which are unimaginable but which were real. And to his dying days, he watched wrestling on TV. His son, Bernie, would walk into his room at the Baycrest nursing home where he happily, almost blissfully lived out his final years, and see him shaking his fists and shouting at the television in total agitation. "I know it is fake," he would tell his son, "but I can't help it."

A 95-year-old Holocaust survivor.

Now imagine 11-year-old boys who didn't know it was fake.

That was what wrestling was to us.

It came on TV on Saturday morning, maybe late morning or early afternoon. We watched on our old black and white TV in the basement. Was it an hour? Was it two? I can't remember. Single matches, pairs, novelty acts, all rolled out in racial and ethnic tropes which would be laughable if they weren't, now looking back, so disturbingly horrible.

Good vs evil.

We all had our heroes. But what really made it a spectacle were the villains. Oh, how we hated the villains.

The Sheik, Giles the Fish Poisson, Killer Kowalski, Mad Dog Vachon and, the biggest villain of all, Abdullah the Butcher, whose signature move was smashing the announcer's chair on the head of his opponent when a round was already over.

Saturday morning wrestling was the highlight of our week. It was the highlight of our lives. Yes, we loved the Canadians and the Expos, but nothing could stir our passions and get our hearts beating out of control more than this televised theatre.

After the show we would take all the cushions from the sofas in the basement to create a soft mat and practice our moves - the sleeper hold, the leg flip, the claw, stopping only to kick my sister out when she came down to snoop on us. Stevie was fake hitting me on the head with the pink plastic chair from my sister's Barbie doll set, crying out "Abdullah the Butcher", when I casually said "You know, he's from Egypt."

In the show, Abdullah the Butcher was portrayed as being from Sudan. But I'm quite sure Stevie Sheen did not know the difference.

In actuality, Abdullah the Butcher was from Niagara Falls, Ontario, and his real name was Lawrence Robert Shreve. But I didn't know that either.

"Yeah," I replied, as I began to replace the cushions on the sofa because I knew if my sister had come down my father wouldn't be far behind. "He's actually friends with my Oncle Emile. They grew up a block from each other in Cairo."

Stevie, who had been on the receiving end of more than a few of my father's lectures, now joined me in trying to put the basement back to its pre-wrestling state. I am sure he did not know any other Egyptians. Did not know that the majority of Jews were not from Egypt. To him, the gibberish language coming out of Abdullah the Butcher's mouth did not seem so dissimilar to the Arabic he heard coming from my aunt's and uncle's mouths. He did not know that Cairo had over ten million inhabitants. So, for all he knew, maybe my Oncle Emile did know Abdullah the Butcher from the old country.

And he would have been perfectly happy to believe me and accept it had I decided to leave it at that.

But I didn't.

Instead, I went on to say "He's coming to my birthday party."

I don't know what Stevie Sheen said to Mike Leese but whatever he said, he decided to change his mind and commit to come to the Zevy house for birthday cake instead of going to Jarry Park to watch the nascent Expos who, on that day, beat Tom Seaver and the Mets 2-0 on a 3 hit gem by Carl Morton.

He wanted to meet Abdullah the Butcher.

Of course, I didn't know Abdullah the Butcher.

My Oncle Emile did not know Abdullah the Butcher.

My mother was thrilled.

Now despite the fact that I said that it didn't really bother me if Stevie Sheen came to my birthday party, it was enough of a thing in our family that when my cousin David, who was four years older than me, came to our house on his blue CCM with a package from his mom to mine, he said to me:

"I heard Stevie Sheen is coming to your party."

We were sitting on the front porch of the house eating sunflower seeds. I was trying to mimic, not all that successfully, his multi seed eat and spit technique, waiting for my mom to prepare the package he would then return to his mom.

"Yeah," I said.

"Hrmph," he replied, his mouth full of sunflower seeds.

"I told him that Abdullah the Butcher was coming," I confessed.

"Is Abdullah the Butcher coming?" He asked, popping eight more seeds into his mouth.

"I don't think so," I replied. "I told him that Oncle Emile knew him from the old country."

"Maybe he sold him a pair of shoes." Oncle Emile was a manager in the shoe department at Eatons.

My favorite part of this story is that David did not think it was such a big deal that I told Stevie Sheen that Abdullah the Butcher was coming for lunch.

He took it in stride.

Kids, I guess he thought, say things.

So, we sat there and spat out sunflower seeds while my mother prepared her package - if I think hard about it I think it was some sort of hair removal formula - and then David said

"Edwin Dweck looks a bit like Abdullah the Butcher."

Now Edwin Dweck was our third cousin on my mother's side.

I think it would be safe to say that he had never been stopped in the street by a young boy who, mistaking him for the famed wrestler, requested an autograph.

But, he was bald.

I hope none of my cousins are reading this because I don't want to disparage their relative but he was the kind of bald man who, because his head was, let's say a little prominent, did not look good bald. Like, say Telly Savalas.

The other thing about Edwin Dweck is that he was not thin.

You see what I did there.

Neither of these things would pass even a tertiary inspection but Edwin Dweck did a third thing which my cousin and I thought might, just might, put us over the top: at family functions he wore, as an homage to the old land, a full length galabeya - a traditional Egyptian and, as luck would have it, Sudanese garment.

He did not look like a wrestler.

But damn if he didn't look Egyptian.

"Is Edwin Dweck coming to your birthday?" Asked David, walking towards his CCM.

"No," I replied. "But I'm about to invite him."

Now I don't know if you understand how extended Jewish Egyptian families work but my mother couldn't just invite Edwin Dweck. If she wanted one Dweck, she had to have them all.

All seventeen.

It should have been 18.

But Edwin never showed.

I tell this story often. I sometimes like to switch up the ending and say he showed up but had lost fifty pounds, was wearing a toupee, and had put on a suit.

Which, I think, is pretty funny

But he just never showed.

Which was probably just as well because I'm not sure we ever thought it through. I caught shit for a few days and neither Stevie or Mike came to my birthday again.

Years later, David and I were at the Toronto Convention Centre working a paint show. In the hall next to us there was a card signing nostalgia show of old-time wrestlers. To tell the truth, most were from slightly later years and we hardly recognized anyone. But there was Abdullah the Butcher. Behind a table with old posters from his heyday behind him. David and I wordlessly made our way over there. Had our pictures taken and autographs signed. I think it cost us $20.

Then David said "Can we buy you lunch?"

And Abdullah the Butcher, Lawrence Shreve, shrugged his shoulder and said "Why not?"

He had a club sandwich with fries. I remember he used up about ten of those mayo containers, diligently, almost daintily, smothering every unexposed corner of the bread.

We talked about hockey. He was a big Detroit Red Wings fan.

Nobody came over to get an autograph. We ate our lunch and went back to our respective conventions.

Every couple of years, David will send me the picture we took of the three of us.

And every time he will send the same caption

"Edwin looks good in this picture."

# LABRADOODLE

Photograph © Susanne906 / pixabay.com

I wouldn't be picking up dog shit with a small plastic bag if I could have remembered if it was garbage day or recycling day.

Check that.

I wouldn't be picking up dog shit with a small plastic bag if I could have just remembered to keep my mouth shut.

The street I live on in Toronto alternates between recycling and garbage each week. I guess every street in Toronto is like that.

On our street, the pickup is on Thursdays.

I am pretty good at remembering on Wednesday night that there is a pickup the next morning. What I am not so good at remembering is whether it is garbage or recycling. I don't know why. I just can't do it.

I can recite all 50 states.

I can, if you give me a minute, even remember all 50 state capitals.

But damn if I can remember if it is garbage or recycling.

So what I usually do is walk over to the neighbours and check which bin they have put out. The recycling bin is blue and the garbage bin is gray but from a distance they kind of look the same, so I have to actually walk over and check for myself. The problem is my neighbour on my left doesn't put out the bin until early morning—which doesn't work for me. And the neighbour on my right—a lovely old Scottish man—has been wrong twice. Which meant four weeks until my overflowing garbage bin gets picked up.

Not a pretty scene.

So I usually end up crossing the street. The family who lives there puts out the bins early and never gets it wrong. They too are a lovely family with two small kids who have been my cross-the-street neighbours for nearly five years.

And I can't remember their names.

Am sure I knew their names at one point and may have even been reminded. But I now had no clue.

Which would be okay if not for the fact that every time I saw the husband, he greeted me with an enthusiastic, "Hey, Ron." Like he was trying to stick it to me.

On that particular Wednesday night, the coast looked clear, so I quickly crossed the street to take a peek—recycling—I fucking knew that and was making a hasty retreat when I heard the screen door open and heard his cheerful, "Hey, Ron."

I had recently defaulted to, "Hey, neighbour," but I knew he knew that I did not know his name and every conversation was just a tiny bit uncomfortable. This one was not any different but it was short and would have been totally innocuous had it not led to me picking up dog shit with a small plastic bag.

He asked me how things were and did not wait for my reply when he announced that they were going to get a dog.

I said, "Oh, yeah."

And he said yeah. The wife wasn't totally on board, but the kids had been really on their case and what with all that was going on and the distance learning and everything, he thought they deserved it even though the wife wasn't totally on board.

And I said, "Oh, yeah."

Then he said they were thinking of a labradoodle.

Did I know what that was?

I did, but he proceeded to tell me anyway.

He finished explaining the hybrid process and the breeder in Milton they were getting it from and then waited for me to say something.

So I said that I was thinking of getting a dog.

Although I wasn't.

"That's great," he said. "Have you decided what kind? Have you lined up a breeder?"

And I said, "I'm not really a breeder type of guy."

Although I was.

"I think I will probably get a rescue. You know what they say— 'adopt, don't shop.'"

I didn't know who said that. I had no idea where I had even heard it.

But, for some reason, it shut him up, and I managed to cross the street back to my house and drag my recycling bin to the curb.

And that should have ended things and kept me far away from dog shit and small inverted plastic bags, and it would have if Mrs. Katsakis had not died.

Mrs. Katsakis was a Greek lady who lived three doors down. She tended her garden most days. In 10 years, I had never spoken to her. I may have waved at her thrice. She lived three doors down. In my world, it was as if she lived in Myanmar.

I did not know her name.

She was the Greek lady who lived three doors down.

I would not have known her name if my neighbour from across the street had not knocked on my door and said, "Hey, Ron, Mrs. Katsakis has died."

I did not know who Mrs. Katsakis was, but I didn't really know any other Greek ladies, and there was no other Greek lady that the neighbour across the street and I had in common, so I was able to piece it together.

I mean, I wasn't a complete idiot.

I'm not sure why my neighbour from across the street thought I needed to know about Mrs. Katsakis. I mean, it was sad and all, but I wasn't sure what it had to do with me. I figured maybe he was collecting some money because I never saw anyone visiting her and she lived in this small bungalow, and even though I didn't know her from Adam, I was happy to do my part, especially if it helped get rid of my neighbour from across the street.

So I said, "Hold on, let me go get my checkbook," even though he hadn't said anything about money and had really only told me that Mrs. Katsakis had died.

I retreated into my house when he said:

"She had a dog."

And I said, "Oh, yeah."

And he said, "Yeah. And I remember you saying you were thinking of getting a dog."

And I said, "Oh, yeah."

And he said, "Yeah. You said you wanted to adopt. Her children live in Vancouver. There is no one to take the dog. So I thought of you. I mean, it feels like serendipity."

Serendipity.

It felt like he was trying to stick it to me.

I asked him what kind of dog.

"A Scottish Terrier. Her name is Olympus."

Olympus. Jesus, Mary and Joseph.


So now I am walking my new dog down the street. Olympus. Stopping from time to time to pick up the shit with a small plastic bag.

I am scooping up the shit when I suddenly remember my neighbour's name:

Ethan.

Fuck.

I should have remembered that.

It is Wednesday night and Ethan has his garbage bins out. I drop the bag of shit into his bin.

Then I cross the street and go home with my dog.

# HANONO

Photograph © Volodymyr Melnyk / 123rf.com

My friend Catherine is at my door. She lives three blocks away. She knows knocking on my door will get my attention faster than a phone call.

"Do you want to play poker tonight?"

I make a face. Catherine plays in a lot of games. I am not crazy about all of her people.

She has anticipated my reaction.

"This is a really good game," she says, countering whatever excuse I was about to make. "One of the partners at my firm, this guy Sami, has a regular home game. Stakes are decent. Really nice guys. Very laid back. Everyone plays well. And he has great desserts."

I have no plans. I have already eaten my frozen pizza. I could really go for some good dessert. I say "Ok."

She says "Come now. Mitchell is already in the car." She knows better than to give me time to change my mind.

I say "Fine. Let me just go pee."

The first thing Mitchell says when I get in the car is "Did Catherine tell you?" Now this could mean a lot of things. Catherine likes to operate on a need to know basis.

Catherine says "I didn't even need to." Turning to me she says "I had a proverbial ace up my sleeve."

I say "You know, you use proverbial way too much. What is your ace?"

"They are Egyptians," she says, knowing my parents were from Egypt. "It is an Egyptian poker game!"

"Really? I used to love playing poker with Egyptians."

And Catherine says to Mitchell "See! I told you he would like it."

An Egyptian poker game. It will give me the chance to use my Arabic.

Now, I don't speak Arabic.

Although my parents were born in Egypt and spoke it fluently, we spoke mainly French and then English in the house. But I used to play in a poker game at the Hemispheres condo building in Hallandale with my late Uncle Henri and his crew of octogenarian Egyptians. So, while I did not know how to speak Arabic, I could play poker in Arabic. I had picked up about two dozen words and expressions.

And I was determined to use one of them.

In truth, the actual poker was played mostly in French with a smattering of English. The cards, neuf de pique, valet de carreaux, were all described in French. The poker hands were a little more polyglot. A full house was a full, although pronounced much like the fava bean dish which was a staple of Egyptian life. A flush was a flush. But a straight was a quinte, which is French, while the rare straight flush, was a quinte flush, a French/English hybrid. Finally, a really lousy hand earned the Arabic designation of 'khara' - just shit. If the actual poker terminology was a little pedestrian, the banter and trash-talk were anything but.

Most of the men in this group had played together since they were teenagers. Their insults, in Arabic and French, had not changed. Which meant they were, by and large, juvenile and puerile. But, with age and maturity came the addition of Arabic idioms and expressions. Some of them were beauties.

I had some favorites. When someone had no clue what they were doing, invariably it was the hapless but loveable Edward Shweck, my uncle Andre would say "Al atrash fil alzifa." Which literally means 'like a deaf man at a wedding'.

Raymond Ben-Simon had the reputation of almost never playing a hand unless he had great cards. So he folded almost all of the time. On those rare occasions when he finally played a hand but lost, Tico was ready with his taunt.

"Sam Sam Sam ou fitir àla bassala."

He fasted fasted fasted and had breakfast with an onion.

Sometimes, the introduction of one idiom would bring a rash of others; seemingly unrelated non-sequiturs.

When my Uncle Henri scooped a pot after making a big bet which went unchallenged, he would wag his finger at me, often I wasn't even in the hand, and say:

"El hekaya labsa melaya."

Literally it means the story is wearing a bedsheet. It is used to say there's more to it than it seems. More to the story than meets the eye.

El hekaya labsa melaya.

I love that. Would make for a great book title.

It would be repeated with nodding heads and wry smiles. They looked a lot like our poker group does when we reminisce about the 1981 Springsteen concert.

There were others, but my all-time favorite was not an idiom. It was a single word. It was usually used, or at least instigated, by my uncle Henri and most often directed at his childhood friend Tico. Tico, may he rest in peace, was a very conservative player and generally took a long time to throw a chip in the pot. My uncle Henri would berate him by saying "Tico, ne sois pas hanono." Tico, don't be cheap. The French sentence with the Arabic last word which was our family trademark.

Hanono.

It was a great word. In a sentence or as a stand-alone. Hanono. I never said it. I never had the guts. It was not my place. Not with this group. I would have loved to have used it in some of my games in Toronto - there was no lack of deserving recipients - but nobody there spoke Arabic. But tonight, I would be playing poker with Egyptians. Now, I am not foolish enough to direct it at complete strangers. Catherine and Mitchell, on the other hand, though truthfully the furthest thing from cheap, are fair game. I just need to find the right moment. I just need one of them to make a bad fold.

Catherine was right. Sami and his three friends, all Egyptians, are really nice and very good poker players to boot. The stakes are reasonable but just large enough to have to make decisions, and everyone plays well and quickly. Along with Sami, there is Sayed, Maurice, and Whalid. Sami is the Uncle Henri of the group. Clearly the leader, he is prone to making big bluffs and even bigger insults. Sayed is the conservative mild-mannered Raymond Ben-Simon. He mostly folds and nervously eats sunflower seeds. I don't think anyone could be Tico but Whalid comes a little close. He has a cloud over his head, loses a bunch of close hands, and is generally the brunt of most of the jokes. Mostly, they call him 'humar', which is donkey. He seethes when he loses a hand and Sami uses an expression I had heard with my own Egyptian group.

"Fokak men nafsak."

Unscrew yourself from yourself.

In other words, take it easy. Sami explains it to the table. "That is a great expression," says Mitchell. Catherine glares at me and I glare back. I am waiting to use my own great expression. But the cards are not helping.

An hour goes by and Catherine and Mitchell have barely folded a hand. Catherine is actually raking in most of the pots and Mitchell is holding his own. I have had plenty of opportunity to throw in a 'mabruk' (congratulations) after a won pot or a 'moosh raali' (not expensive) after calling a bet, or an 'abadan' (I have nothing), when caught in a bluff, but no, I have abstained. I am locked in to 'hanono'.

By hour two, I am getting a little desperate. When the moment comes, it does not even rise to the level of anything. It is just a fold. There is a small raise and everyone calls except for Catherine, who folds and a second later asks "Where is the restroom?" But between the time she said "fold" and the time she said "Where is the restroom?" I managed to triumphantly shout out "hanono!"

Everyone looks at me. Each with a quizzical look on their face. So I say it again: "hanono."

Catherine says "What does that mean?"

And I reply "It means cheap in Arabic."

And Sami says "I don't think it does."

And I say, to the four Egyptians "Yes it does." And, thinking maybe my pronunciation was off, repeat it again slowly: "ha-no-no".

Sayed, who is a pediatrician says "I don't think that is a word in Arabic." He says it in a very kind and gentle manner, like he is speaking to one of his patients.

I say "My family is from Cairo. From Heliopolis. I used to hear it all the time."

Sayed says "I am also from Heliopolis. But I have never heard that word."

And Sami says "I'm sorry. In Arabic cheap is 'Rakhis'. There are a few other adjectives and colloquialisms. But I have never heard of hanono. Sorry."

I say "Oh. I'm sorry."

And Catherine says "I'm not cheap, I just had to go to the bathroom."

The table falls quiet.

Sami says maybe this would be a good time to have dessert.

Again, Catherine was right. The desserts are delicious. They had been made by Sami himself, apparently the chef in the family. The table has pistachio and honey-laden Konafa, basbousa, which is semolina cake soaked in syrup, and zalabya, the fried balls of dough which my cousins and I knew would be waiting for us every time we visited our Tante Racheline. Were it not for the hanono debacle I would tell Sami and Sayed, the Heliopolis native, that dessert is almost as good as the pastries at Om Met Kek on Rue Ismaili Pasha.

The game resumes without incident. It is still fun but the air has gone out of the room. In the car on the way home Catherine says "What was that all about?"

I say "I don't know."

She says "I thought you could speak some words in Arabic?"

And I say "So did I."

The next day, I call my Tante Odette.

"Comment ça va?" I ask.

As usual, she answers "Zay el zift, merci." I am shit, thank you.

"Dis moi, tell me. When Henri called Tico hanono. What did it mean?"

"Hanono? Hanono meant he was calling him cheap."

I say "In Arabic?"

Odette says "No."

"Not in Arabic?"

And Odette says "No."

"Is it French?" Although I know it isn't.

And Odette says "No."

I say "So what language is it?"

Odette says "What language? It isn't any language. It is his name."

"Whose name?" I ask.

She says "Marcel Hanono. He was at school with your father and uncle in Cairo. Il était très avars. He was very cheap."

Marcel Hanono. My all-time favorite Arabic word is not Arabic at all.

I say "Ok thanks."

She says "Yallah bye," and hangs up.

I sit in silence for a few seconds then scream out "Fuuuuuuck!!"

I just hope it isn't someone's name.

# TWENTY CENT WINGS

Photograph © Brent Hofacker / 123rf.com

My uncle called me into his office. He did not look happy. He did not look happy at all. He had one bad eye so it was never clear if he was looking at you. But what I couldn't see, I could definitely feel.

He opened a folder, I could see it was my expense report folder, removed an item and pushed it in my direction.

"What is this?" he asked.

I picked it up and looked at it. It was a lunch receipt. From Gabby's Roadhouse in Brampton.

"I marked it down," I replied defensively. "It was lunch with Derek Dawson. You told me to take him to lunch."

Derek Dawson was the paint line supervisor for a huge manufacturer. We had been trying to get their account for years. I was the paint salesman in charge of the account.

My uncle snatched the receipt from me and inspected it carefully.

"I told you to take him to lunch. $6.99. What could you possibly eat for $6.99?"

"We shared chicken wings," I said. "Honey garlic. He said he liked honey garlic."

"Chicken wings?" My uncle looked like he was going to lose it. "It could be the biggest account in all of Ontario and you took him for chicken wings?"

"I asked him what he wanted. He said honey garlic chicken wings from Gabby's. We shared a dozen."

"You shared? You didn't even let him have his own plate?"

"Well the wings at Gabby's are really fat. I think that is why he likes them. Plus they come with fries. I only had four. Am sure he was full."

"$6.99?"

"It was 20-cent chicken wing day."

"20 cents for chicken wings." I was getting worried about my uncle. He had a heart condition.

"The Wednesday special."

"The Wednesday special?" Now he was only repeating what I was saying. He inspected the receipt again.

"You drank Coke?"

"Yes. We each had a Coke. Gabby's has free refills. He said he liked that."

"You couldn't have a beer?"

Salesmen all over the world were being berated for three martini lunches and I was about to be fired because I only drank Coke.

"$6.99? You submitted a receipt for $6.99?"

"I think I may have tipped $3. But I didn't expense it. I think I may have left a 10."

"$6.99. $6.99." My uncle couldn't get over it.

I was about to get fired for submitting too small an expense account.

"It was a good lunch." I was almost in tears. "We talked about fly fishing."

"Fly fishing?"

"Yeah. He likes to fish."

My uncle, for what I was sure was the first time in his life, was at a loss for words. Which was a good thing, because the next words out of his mouth would have been bad for me. But then the phone rang and there was a crisis in the lab and I slinked out of his office.

My uncle and my father both worked at Sherwin Williams in Montreal. It was a huge paint manufacturer. They were both chemical engineers. My father got out in the early 70s and got a job in Ottawa with the government. My uncle though stayed longer and he became one of the pioneers in developing a new dry paint, powder coating, application which was applied with an electrostatic charge and then baked in an oven. Unlike wet paint, which creates sludge which had to be disposed, the powder paint could be reused and recycled. At the late age of 50, my uncle decided to leave Sherwin Williams and open up his own company. He called it Protech Chemicals. He had two partners. Then one of his partners dropped out. My father came up with the money and became a small silent partner. He remained a very silent partner.

My mom, however, would occasionally have something to say. Mostly asking her brother to give me my job back.

That kind of thing.

When I wrote, "Even though my uncle fired me three times, he was still my favorite uncle," my cousin David, who built the business with his father, was very quick to contact me in order to point out an error in that statement.

"David," I argued. "Your dad was my favorite uncle."

"Yes," he agreed. "I know he was."

"And I was fired three times," I continued.

And he said, "That is where I take issue."

I said, "Why?"

"Because," he explained, "you say you were fired three times. But you should have said you were ONLY fired three times."

Ah. Yes. He had a point. He had a good point. There are a bunch of examples. But I knew what he was talking about. He was talking about Ashley Broodmore.

Ashley Broodmore is not somebody's name. It is the name of a company. The company makes electrical boxes. We have all seen them. The grey boxes which house our fuses. But they made these big industrial electrical boxes. The ones you see in the back of a plant. They painted them with a grey paint. Many of the names of the paint colors we sold were crowned by my uncle and cousin. For example, the bright high-gloss orange paint we sold was called Philly Orange as an homage to the Philadelphia Flyers. My uncle, although a lifelong Montreal Canadiens fan, had a *joie de vivre* sense of humor.

The grey we sold Ashley Broodmore, however, had a name and designation which came straight from the electrical industry. It was called ASA 49 Grey.

It had many specifications. Durability, color, that kind of thing. One of the specifications was gloss. A lay person, one who buys paint for their wall, understands that a paint can either be matte, that is no or low gloss, or high gloss.

Ashley Broodmore's ASA 49 Grey had a specification of 35-39 gloss. Which is not quite matte and not quite gloss. And they had a high-fangled gloss meter to measure it when the pieces came out of the oven.

One day, the measurement was 41.

They halted production.

They called our office and said get somebody in here immediately.

That somebody was me.

Now the thing was, I didn't get the message right away.

Because my afternoon tennis game had gone into a third set.

So, by the time I retrieved my seven increasingly irritated messages, went home to shower and change into a suit, and drove the two hours to London, Ontario, it was already very late afternoon and the entire production line had been shut down for the entire day.

They were waiting for me in the conference room. The President and about 30 other people. I made my apologies, did not mention losing in a third set tiebreaker, and asked what I could do to help.

Someone handed me a piece of grey metal. It looked good. Perfect application.

"Do you have a gloss meter?"

I said I did. It was in the trunk of my Pontiac Phoenix. I went to the parking lot, opened my trunk, rummaged through the tennis rackets and balls, and retrieved it. I then went back to the conference room and did a reading.

41.

I asked for another piece.

41.

I asked for one more.

41.

"Forty one." I declared authoritatively. "Very consistent."

The President was not amused. "Our specs are 35-39," he said very firmly. "Your paint is off spec and it shut down our operation. Now what are you going to do about it?"

This was an easy one. We would manufacture a new batch overnight and ship it express the first thing in the morning.

It was a no-brainer.

Ashley Broodmore was a huge account.

It was a total no-brainer.

It was exactly what I should have said.

But I didn't.

Because I was in a bad mood.

I really hate losing in a third set tiebreaker.

And also driving two hours in rush hour to get dressed down over something that is not discernible to the naked eye. And about having to sell powder paint for a living.

So instead I said, "It's just an electrical box." To the President of the company who made electrical boxes and 30 of his employees.

He didn't say anything. I suspect he was in shock. I took the silence as a sign I could soldier on. "It is just an electrical box," I repeated. "It goes in the back of the plant. Nobody will ever be able to tell the difference."

The President nodded and thanked me for coming in. He then called my uncle and told him to never send me in ever again.

The most shocking part of the story is we didn't lose the account and I didn't lose my job.

Well, I did, but that was later.

I had written my first children's book by then and was devoting most of my time to what would become my first company. It wasn't really until I had my own company and my own lazy employees that I really understood my uncle.

So the third firing was the easiest. We both knew it was time.

Derek Dawson and I talked about fly fishing. I have never fished but I had read a few books. *A River Runs Through It*. Also, as you may have already guessed, I can spin a tale. I never really liked talking about paint. I would drop by the plant, he would take a cigarette break and we would stand outside near the loading docks and talk about fishing. Which lure to use. Which were the best fishing spots. We never mentioned paint. I discovered that selling was about connecting with people.

I was good at that.

It was the biggest account I ever landed. The competition never had a chance after that.

Go figure.

Fly fishing.

I actually got a few big accounts that year.

"We had a good year," I said to my uncle.

"6.99," he retorted. I would like to think he was joking. But I don't really think so. He knew I was just phoning it in. Just biding my time. I can't really blame him.

Selling paint was not my thing. I went on to discover other things. I am still discovering.

We got along much better when we were just uncle and nephew. We played poker. I took him shopping. Then back to return the things he had bought. I let him pick the restaurants. My choices were always shit.

We complained about employees. We reminisced about customers. About sales trips.

zAbout the time he told the not-pregnant Lisa that smoking was not good for the baby. I boasted about my sales, my numbers, my successes. I picked up the check.

I call my cousin David while I am writing this story and ask how much we used to sell the ASA 49 Grey for.

We.

25 years later, and I am still saying "we."

Fired three times and I am still saying "we."

"You writing the Ashley Broodmore story?" he asks. I say, "Yeah."

"It's just an electrical box."

"Yeah, I dunno. Kinda sounds like something I might have said."

"You were so bad."

"I know. So bad. At least it produced some good stories."

"You tell the chicken wing story?"

"Yeah," I reply.

"Derek Dawson." He remembers the name right away.

"I'm impressed," I say.

"Are you fucking kidding me! Gabby's Roadhouse. $6.99."

"It was a monster account," I say.

"Yes," he agrees. "It was a monster."

"Free Coke refills," I say.

"You ever fish with Derek Dawson?" I didn't answer. He knew I didn't.

"Classic story. You wrote it up?"

"Yeah."

"Send it to me."

So I do. I don't hear back but a few days later a FedEx arrives at my house. I open it up and there are three loonies—three dollars—and a note.

It is from my cousin David.

"This covers the tip."

The last meal I had alone at a restaurant with my uncle was at a roadside joint in Hallandale Florida called Big Daddy Flanigan's. It was a liquor store which doubled as a type of diner. Ribs, burgers. That kind of thing. It was a dive and it wasn't clear why he liked it, but he insisted it was good. We had gone on some sort of wild goose chase looking for a $99 suit he had heard advertised on TV. We stopped at Flanigan's for lunch on the way back. We both had beers and I ordered the fish tacos. My uncle looked sideways at the waitress. I think he was trying to read her name tag.

"Justine," I said out loud.

"Let me ask you this, Justine," said my uncle. "Do you have 20-cent wings?" he said it with a straight face.

Justine was unfazed.

"$9.99 for a dozen," she replied.

"It comes with fries?"

"Yes, sir."

"Okay. I will have wings."

"Which flavor would you like?"

"Do you have honey garlic?"

Justine said yes.

"Okay. A dozen honey garlic."

Justine left. I looked over at my uncle. His face did not betray a thing.

Then he slowly lifted his Corona. It was really only a few inches above the table.

"To Derek Dawson," he said.

"To Derek Dawson," I replied.

# DRIVING A TRACTOR

Photograph © andreas160578 / pixabay.com

I have never told this story before.

The reason I never tell this story is because it requires the reader to believe two things which, all things being fair, are frankly a little hard to believe.

The first thing is having once slept with a woman who later went on to become a Sports Illustrated swimsuit model.

I will let you try to absorb that. A bit hard to swallow. I mean, I know, even if you are feeling generous and are willing to give me the benefit of the doubt, it feels more than a little outside of the realms of possibility. I understand. I don't blame you. I have trouble believing it too. It is why I never ever tell this story. Because, if you have trouble believing the first thing, there is absolutely no way you can possibly wrap your head around the second. Which is: I can drive a tractor.

In 1981, I went to Israel in order to spend some time on a kibbutz learning to speak Hebrew. The program—it was called Ulpan—was very popular amongst young North American Jews and I saw it as an opportunity to learn a little more about the country where I had been born.

The Ulpan program was set up as learning Hebrew for half the day and volunteering doing manual labour on the kibbutz for the other half.

The Ulpan office was in Tel Aviv on Hayarkon, and I immediately hit the jackpot by being assigned to Kibbutz Yotvata.

Yotvata was a legendary kibbutz in the Israeli Negev Desert and was famous for their dairy products. Although crazy hot in the summer, it was the perfect place to be in the fall and winter months which were now ahead of me.

Yotvata is only a few minutes from Eilat and is on the southern tip of the country. It was as far as you could go. I got dropped off on the side of the road after a five-hour bus ride. The scenery, the combination of the desert and Jordanian mountains in the background, was breathtaking. I lugged my backpack down the long kibbutz drive and was directed to the Ulpan program residences. Although, army barracks might have been a better term.

I walked in and met the three guys who would be my roommates. They were not in good spirits. They had just learned of their volunteer work assignments and they were not happy.

"Fucking dairy at 3:00 am in the morning," spat out Hershel, who was from West Bloomfield, Michigan. "Fucking 3:00 am!"

The other two, who had still not bothered to introduce themselves, did not speak. But they both looked very sullen

The dairy. That did not sound great. I'm not sure what I had envisioned. I guess standing on a ladder picking oranges.

One of the other two stuck his hand out and introduced himself. "Joel Gordon. I'm from Rochester. I heard the smell was disgusting. I heard two of the girls had thrown up."

Hershel said, "You better get your ass over to the volunteer office. Go meet Arik."

"Arik?"

"Arik Ben Simon. He is a real asshole."

Joel Gordon said he would show me the way. We didn't speak as we walked down the narrow path to the kibbutz volunteer office. Joel stopped at the doorway, not wanting to incur Arik's wrath again, and gently nudged me into the office.

Arik Ben Simon looked like the poster book of an Israeli kibbutznik. He had a scruffy beard, a round hat, and was wearing blue dirty overalls. He looked like a man who had never owned, much less, worn a tie. If he had one, it was likely only to strangle people.

He pointed to a chair and told me to sit. He had still not looked up at me. When he did finally look up, it was to give me a speech. It was clear it was not the first time he had delivered it.

"I don't like Ulpan. You want to learn Hebrew. Learn it at home. This is a kibbutz. We work the land. We produce food. I don't have time to hold hands and sing kumbaya with soft North Americans who are here for a genuine Israeli experience."

When he said 'experience' he used air quotes. But when he did it looked like he was scratching someone's eyes out.

He continued without missing a beat.

"The Ulpan program people all work in the dairy. You know why they work in the dairy?"

I was only 21, but I knew a rhetorical question when I heard one, so I kept my mouth shut.

"I'll tell you why they work in the dairy. Because we have determined that is where they can do the least amount of damage. Stacking and unstacking crates. Do you understand?"

Again, I chose to stay silent.

But this time the question was not rhetorical.

"Gever gever. Are you mute? Can you not speak? I asked you if you understood?"

I nodded my head yes. I couldn't speak. Partly because I was scared to death and partly because I had a mouth full of kaak—the hard Egyptian sesame mini bagel—which my mother had packed for me in a small plastic bag for my flight and which I had begun to eat nervously while Arik was midway through his diatribe.

"What is that?" he demanded to know. "What are you eating?"

I held up the plastic bag which still held three kaak.

He extended his big meaty hand and I deposited the bag.

He turned the bag upside down and examined the bag from different sides. Then he reached into the bag and held it up to the light. Like a jeweller examining a diamond.

And then the bear turned into a lamb.

He looked at me and said, "Kaak."

My speech came back and I said, "My mother made them."

He nodded his head and then gently said, "Efshar. Is it okay if I have one?"

I hadn't started my first Hebrew class but I knew enough words to answer, "Beitach!" Of course you can.

Arik ate the first kaak and then the next two without asking.

He licked his lips.

"You know how long it has been since I have had kaak?"

I shook my head no.

"A long time. These are almost as good as my mother's. Almost."

I just sat there and said nothing.

He opened a folder and held up a file

"Aaron Zevy. Ottawa, Canada. Okay, Aaron Zevy. Tomorrow at 7:00 am you work with me. Bananot. Yallah, bye."

The bananas was the kibbutz's cash crop. Every banana was shipped for export. We never ate a single banana in the dining room.

This is how it worked.

Each banana tree had one bunch of bananas. A volunteer would stand underneath the bunch while an Israeli with a huge machete would chop off the bunch. The trees were short and the bunches hung low so you could cradle the bunch on your shoulder until the Israeli chopped it off. You would then walk the bunch of bananas into the flatbed trailer behind the tractor. Someone was supposed to move the tractor from time to time as we moved further away down the row of banana trees.

But nobody ever did.

There were two Dutch girls, Ingrid and Bridgette, who took an immediate dislike to me and my work ethic. They could put a bunch of bananas on each shoulder and make three trips back and forth to the flatbed during the same time it took me to make one trip with one bunch. I heard their grumbling. It was Dutch but I know grumbling when I hear it.

By mid-morning, I was beginning to realize that my mother could not possibly make enough kaaks to keep Arik from wanting to take the machete to my head. Or at least banishing me to the dairy.

But you should never underestimate the power of Fernande Zevy's kaaks.

Arik pulled me aside and asked, "Tell me, Aaron Zevy. Can you drive steek?"

I had, up to that point, not even driven a car. Much less one which had a stick shift. Let alone a tractor. I had driven a bumper car at the amusement park.

But, I thought, how hard could it be?

But this was no time to be timid.

"Are you kidding, I got a tractor for my bar mitzvah."

Arik swore in Arabic and motioned me to follow him into the cab of the tractor. Turned out I was a natural.

Go figure.

And so, for three months of the winter of 1981 at Kibbutz Yotvata in the Israeli desert, I drove a Massey Ferguson model 1084 tractor. I got pretty good too.

I'd like to say that the Dutch girls came around and we all became life-long friends.

But they didn't.

Can't really blame them though. One time I lost control of the tractor and ran over Ingrid's foot.

Ingrid Van der Hooven. Her foot healed and she became a model. Even landed in the pages of the Sports Illustrated Swimsuit edition.

Oh, did I say slept with? My bad. I meant ran over.

But seriously, how else was I going to get you to read a story about driving a tractor?

# OUR FATHER, OUR KING

Photograph © AJ Butler

This story is about the time my car was stolen from my driveway. There is a chance I stray a little and talk about religion, observance of Jewish rituals, and belief in God. If I do stray it is likely because the car was stolen on Yom Kippur—the holiest day of the year on the Jewish calendar. It is a day of fasting and praying. A day of asking for forgiveness from your fellow man. A day spent at the synagogue with fellow Jews. Am not sure yet which direction this story will take. Am just letting you know it might meander from the automative to matters theological. If it does, there is a chance it is because when I opened my front door that Yom Kippur morning and discovered my Audi SQ5 was missing, I was on my way not to synagogue but to breakfast. I would like to tell you my car was stolen by a sophisticated gang of car thieves who prowled the neighborhood at night casing expensive German automobiles.

I would like to. But I can't. Besides, we both know it isn't true. And what kind of relationship do we have if it isn't one based on honesty and mutual respect? It was stolen because I left the keys inside the car.

I opened the door, saw my car was gone, and immediately understood it had been stolen because I had gone to bed the night before and stupidly left the keys in the car.

You know how sometimes you open the door and your car isn't on the driveway and you feel sick to your stomach and your heart drops because you think it has been stolen until you remember you parked it on the street because you had a couch delivered and the moving guys asked you to move your car because they were worried they might scratch it while moving the couch but then you forgot to move it back and then you see it on the street and breathe a sigh of relief?

Well it wasn't like that.

Or when you fly back from Florida and land at midnight and customs takes forever and it is freezing but you left your coat in your car and you are on the third level of the parking garage at Pearson freezing your ass off and can't find your car although you are sure you parked it near the elevator on level three and then you give one of the attendants driving around in a golf cart $20 to drive you up and down the aisles until you finally remember you flew down on Air Canada but flew back on WestJet and you are in the wrong terminal?

It wasn't like that.

I opened the door, saw the car was missing, and immediately realized it had been stolen.

I'm not saying it was a good feeling. But I was spared the sick feeling of thinking it had been stolen. I knew it had been stolen.

I went back into the house and called the police and my insurance company. I told them both the truth. I had left the key overnight in the car.

I then called my friend Carainn and told her my car had been stolen. She said, "Oh my god, is there anything I can do?" I said, "Actually, I would appreciate a ride because I had to go pick up lox." She said she would be right over and she was. I directed her to Kristapsons on Yonge Street. It has the best smoked salmon and I had told Caroline, my sister-in-law, I would pick up the order she had placed for the break fast meal she was having at her house because the store was in my neighborhood.

When we got there Carainn began to laugh. I said, "What's so funny." She said, "I thought you had to buy new locks because your car had been stolen."

"No, not locks, lox."

She said, "I get it now."

I take an Uber to my brother's house. I have the lox. I don't mind taking an Uber. For a few minutes I flirt with the notion of not getting a new car. But that is crazy talk. I get to my brother's house and everyone is busy getting dressed and ready to go to synagogue for the last evening prayer—it is called Ne'ila—before the end of the 25-hour fast.

I have not fasted nor gone to synagogue in 20 years.

I used to go to synagogue when I was young. My father would take me. It was an Ashkenazi shul in the West Island of Montreal. Beth Tikvah. The house of hope. The rabbi was Rabbi Zeitz. We weren't Ashkenazi. Egyptian Jews are Sephardic. My cousin David, Alain Tibul and I were the only three Sephardic kids. When our fathers were called to the Torah for an 'aliyah,' we, as the sons, had to stand while our fathers read that portion of the Torah. It was the Sephardic tradition. My heart would pound the whole time. Everyone in the congregation was sitting but me. Then during my bar mitzvah lessons I would often get the honor of leading the conclusion of the services. Ein Keloheinu, Aleinu, Vinemar, and then Adon Olam. Think of it as the three-song encore at the end of a concert. There was a silent prayer between Aleinu and Vinemar and Rabbi Zeitz would give a signal with a nod of his head.

And then my bar mitzvah. The parsha was Emor. I still know my maftir off by heart. I can still recite my haftorah. *Vehakohanim halvim.*

I knew my stuff. And I believed in it.

And then things changed. Perhaps maturity. Perhaps the advent of critical thinking. Maybe girls. Maybe sports. I say it was because they changed the tunes of my songs. Without the familiar tunes, they were just prayers. And then there is the whole belief thing.

My brother asks if I want to go to shul (synagogue) for Ne'ila. He does it by rote. Like my mother before him and my father before her. I have said no for 20 years.

Today I say yes.

My brother doesn't bat an eye. He looks me up and down and says, "Let me get you a suit."

I change in the bathroom. I eschew the jacket and tie and stick with the dress shirt and pants. Our feet are the same size so I slip on a pair of his dress loafers.

My nieces are abuzz.

"Wait. What? Uncle Ronnie is going to shul? WTF?"

I don't think this has anything to do with my car being stolen on Yom Kippur.

I don't.

I just decide I am going to shul.

Believe what you want. I just want to hear some tunes.

I go to shul. There is a lot of standing. Someone hands me a book but I don't open it. I don't really get prayer. I see a woman I used to date. I don't wave. And then it's over.

The police call while I am having my sister-in-law's famous butternut squash soup back in the house. We have it in coffee cups. I guess maybe because there aren't enough soup bowls to go around. They have found my car. Wow, that didn't take long. It was abandoned in a strip plaza in North York. It was locked. They ask if I can bring a spare key to 41 division. They will then call me in 48 hours after doing their investigation. It is likely some kid took it on a joy ride. I wonder if my golf clubs are still in the trunk. The break fast has great food. I tell my lox/locks story. I tell my I-left-the-key-in-the-car story. I don't care. I have done worse.

The cops call again two days later. I can pick up my car but I should order a tow truck because the battery is now dead. I call a tow company and meet Desmond and his truck at the police car impound lot. Desmond is a tall skinny Jamaican. He has a Toronto Raptors cap, slightly askance, perched on the top of his head. The battery is not dead. "Battery not dead, man," he mutters to me when the car starts right up without a boost. I shrug my shoulders. I just want to get out of there. A policeman tells me to tow it to the Audi dealership and have them conduct a thorough once-over.

"You can't believe what these guys can do to cars they have stolen. Sugar in the gas tank. They piss in the back seat."

The car looks fine to me but I ride with Desmond to the Audi dealership. I have already decided I am going to trade it in. This car has bad karma. Desmond goes on a rant about thieves and how the city is going to hell in a hand basket.

I don't tell him I left the keys in the car.

There is a long silence and I get uncomfortable. All of a sudden I tell him it was stolen on Yom Kippur—the holiest day of the year.

Desmond asks if he thinks it is a sign. I tell him I don't know. I ask Desmond if he believes in God.

He hesitates for a second and then replies,

"Here's the thing. If there is a god and I believe in him then that is good. But if there is a god and I don't believe in him, then it could be bad for me. I could go to hell. You see? But if there is no god then it makes no difference if I believe in him. It costs me nothing. You see what I'm getting at? Believing is the better deal man. You see?"

I do see. Desmond, in his own way, has just described Pascal's Wager.

He drops the car off in the Audi parking lot. I sign the Visa charge and give him a big tip. He says, "Nice car," and leaves.

I do a quick inspection of the car. My CDs are gone. The thief must have been a Shlomo Artzi fan. My golf clubs are in the trunk but the golf bag has been emptied of its golf balls. A coat is missing. But otherwise it looks more or less okay.

I look in the back seat and find a gym bag which does not belong to me. On top of the gym bag is a pack of cigarettes.

I don't smoke.

I go to the office and the salesman is preparing a new deal offer. I call the police and tell them about the bag.

I don't mention the cigarettes.

The cop says, "Look in the bag, call us if you find a gun." I get it. They got the car back. They have bigger fish to fry.

There is zero chance I am going to look in the bag.

The salesman asks how many miles on the car. I say I don't know. He says, "Let's go take a look." So we walk together to the car in the parking lot. I say, "Do you mind doing me a favor? There is a bag in the back seat which does not belong to me. Would you mind taking a look?"

He says sure. He opens the gym bag and hands it to me.

There is no gun. There is a book binder. In the binder is a high school student identification card.

I feel a little bad for the kid. He was likely walking up the street trying car doors to see if any were unlocked. Maybe hoping for some spare change or something more valuable. He comes to my car and sees that the schmuck owner has left the keys in the car. What is he supposed to do? So he takes it on a joy ride. Then parks it. Locks the door. Goes to bed with the thought of driving it again. Get up the next morning and discovers the car, his gym bag, and his student ID are now gone. He's home waiting for the cops to knock on his door.

It's got to be a shit feeling.

I reach into the bag, grab the ID, and slip it into my back pocket. The salesman asks what I want to do with the bag. I say he can throw it out.

I pick up my brand new Audi a few days later. The salesman says I can get the type of key you have to insert into the ignition. I say no. I've got this.

I drive my new car to my friend Harry's house. It is poker night. I tell my stolen car story. I tell them about the high school ID I found in the bag. I don't tell them I still have it in my back pocket. The guys at my poker game say they would have gone to speak to his parents. Teach the kid a lesson. But I think that is crazy. Kid definitely learned his lesson. I go home up $48 driving my brand new Audi... I can buy new golf balls, a new coat, and replace the Shlomo Artzi CDs. I park my car in my driveway, lock the car, and put the keys in the little cubby above the stove. I take the ID out of my pocket and actually look at it for the first time. A generic Canadian name. Wire-rimmed glasses. A bad picture day haircut and a sheepish grin. He could be any kid. I find scissors in my tool drawer in the kitchen and cut the card into four strips. Like a waitress does to your credit card when they get instructions from Visa. I throw the four strips in the garbage.

The Yom Kippur prayer I had wanted to hear was Avinu Malkeinu. Our Father Our King. It is a hypnotic litany asking for forgiveness. The chorus is repeated with rhyming words. It soars and dips as we sway and our voices get a little louder with each new verse.

*Our Father Our King*
*Hear our prayer*
*We have sinned before thee*
*Have compassion upon us and on our children*

You can't get it out of your head. It stays with you for a week after the high holy days are over.

It is recited at the end of the Ne'ila services. It was worth the wait. It was like I remembered it.

When I get home from poker I go online and look it up on YouTube.

There are a lot of versions available. Barbara Streisand singing to Bill Clinton and Shimon Peres. An Orthodox choir. Even a 14-minute extended live version by Phish which will blow your mind. I listen to each one. Then I listen to them again.

*Avinu Malkeinu*
*Our Father Our King*

I get up to go to the bathroom at 3:00 am. Before going back to my room, I open my front door to check if my car is still there. It is.

Then I go back to bed.

# MY MOTHER

84 years.

There is a lifetime of stories to choose from which illustrate her kindness, consideration and character. But I don't need to go back that far.

Let me just tell you about this month.

We flew back from Florida on April 1st and my mother made a point of telling me that she was not going to eat on the plane. She told me on the car ride to the airport, she told me in the lounge at the gate, and she told me as we took off from Fort Lauderdale to Toronto. When the stewardess came by with the choices for dinner, my mom perked up and said, *"Montre moi le menu."* Show me the menu.

The choices were beef, ravioli, or chicken curry. When the stewardess came back, I chose the ravioli and my mother said to the stewardess, "I'll have the chicken, but I don't like curry. How else can you make it?"

She had the chicken curry and proclaimed it to be the most tender piece of chicken she had ever had. When she finished her dinner, she began wildly motioning in order to get the attention of the stewardess.

"Mom," I said, trying desperately to avoid a scene, "just tell me what you want and I'll get it for you." "*Que ce que ça te regard,*" she said, what is to you, "*Je ve lui parler.*" She finally caught the stewardess' eye, and she came over as I tried to shrink into my seat.

"Yes, ma'am," said the stewardess.

"My compliments to the chef," replied my mom with a smile.

That was my mother.

I pick her up at her condo on the way to the first seder. I have called from the road. "Come on down?" she says with no preamble. Yes. This is our ritual. She is waiting in the lobby and makes her way to my car with her walker—her Cadillac, she calls it. The ritual continues. Walker thrown in the trunk. She sidles into the front seat and declares, like she has every time before, "*Il fait un froid de diable.*" It could be 92 degrees, but even the slightest breeze merits the wearing of a coat. I ease away from the circular driveway and the ritual continues. "Wait until I put on my seatbelt." The drive to Dov and Caroline's from the condo is a short one. But a silent journey is not an option. My mother likes to talk. And it is not a regular conversation. It starts with a series of non sequiturs. Free verse like the poets of San Francisco in the 60s. The continuation of a conversation from earlier in the day. From earlier in the week. This day, she does not disappoint. It is a beauty.

"Odette," she declares, "does not like Mr. Wonderful." It is less hard to decipher. We used to watch Shark Tank together. I would often check my answering machine and the message from my mom was "Shark Tank at 8:00." And no more. She was always trying to connect with you. "Tiger Woods, is taking a break from golf." Click. That was her message. Her radio in both Florida and Toronto was tuned, not to classical, not to the CBC, but to Top 40 so she could share the music with her grandchildren.

That was my mother.

At the seders, after pronouncing for the umpteenth time that she, too, had left Egypt, she took her turn reading the Haggadah and could not resist adding a dramatic flare in order to get a laugh from the table. She mispronounces words. She does it on purpose. I am convinced of it. Every day she watched Wheel of Fortune at 7:00 and Jeopardy at 7:30. But she insisted on pronouncing it "Jopordy." On purpose. It was her thing. "I make you laugh, don't I," she proclaimed proudly. And then, without missing a beat, would sternly announce, "*Il y a une fenetre ouverte quelque par.*" "There's a window open somewhere."

That was my mother.

And just a week ago, she called to tell me that the wifi was not working in her condo. I said that one of the girls would come by later in order to help her. But my mom was never a big fan of later. My mom was a big fan of now. It was Chol HaMoed and she wanted to FaceTime with her family in Israel. So she got on the phone and spent an hour with Rogers Customer Service and figured it out herself. And then called me to let me know. An 84-year-old from Cairo who, a year earlier, had never even heard of the word wifi.

In the coming hours, days, weeks, months, and yes, years, many of us in this room will continue to share stories about this remarkable woman. And we will say that she lived a full life. And, in part, we will be right. A life that took her from Egypt to Israel to Canada. A life in which she raised a family and traveled to exotic parts of the world. A life with children, grandchildren, and yes, even a great grandchild. A life surrounded by friends and one in which she left a lasting impression on everyone she met. And I know it is true. And I also know that she got a Kindle at 80, and an iPad at 82. And that although she was not always clear on the difference between Facebook and FaceTime, that she would have figured out how to use the great scientific and technological discoveries which lay ahead of us if it were a way to get her closer and connect to her family, her children, grandchildren, great grandchildren, and all the people she loved and who loved her.

And so, if we believe in *haolam haba*, the world to come, I would like to think of my mom in a room with my dad, she has asked Hashem to please turn down the air conditioning, and she is watching Jopordy, and on the phone with technical support, trying to figure out a way to send a message to the people she loved.

Because, that is my mother.

And I will miss her.

# ABOUT THE AUTHOR

Aaron Zevy is the author of *Almost the Truth: Stories and Lies, The Bubbe Meise and Other Stories*, and *Not Book Club Material*.

*Schlepping Across the Nile: Collected Stories*, is his fourth book.